# Sophist

# PLATO

# Sophist

Translated,
with Introduction and Notes, by
NICHOLAS P. WHITE

Hackett Publishing Company
Indianapolis/Cambridge

Copyright © 1993 by Hackett Publishing Company, Inc.

All rights reserved

Printed in the United States of America

99   98   97   96                    2   3   4   5   6   7

Cover design by Listenberger Design & Associates

Text design by Dan Kirklin

For further information, please address

Hackett Publishing Company, Inc.
P.O. Box 44937
Indianapolis, Indiana 46244-0937

Library of Congress Cataloging in Publication Data

Plato.
[Sophist. English]
Sophist/Plato; translated, with introduction and notes, by Nicholas P. White.
    p.   cm.
Includes bibliographical references.
ISBN 0-87220-203-8.   ISBN 0-87220-202-X (pbk.)
1. Sophists (Greek philosophy)—Early works to 1800.
2. Methodology—Early works to 1800.   3. Ontology—Early works to 1800.   4. Meaning (Philosophy)—Early works to 1800.   I. White, Nicholas P., 1942–      .   II. Title.
B384.A6W48   1993
183'.1—dc20                                                    93-5792
                                                                CIP

The paper used in this publication meets the minimum
requirements of American National Standard for
Information Sciences—Permanence of Paper for Printed
Library Materials, ANSI Z39.48-1984.
                                ∞

# Contents

# Introduction

## 1. The *Sophist* and Modern Philosophy

Plato's *Sophist* has held special significance in recent decades. Of all of his works it has seemed to speak most directly to philosophical interests of modern American and British philosophers. Much of the most sophisticated Platonic scholarship has been aimed at interpreting it.

There have been three main reasons for this. The most important is that the work is open to a largely antimetaphysical interpretation. Much twentieth-century British and American philosophy has been hostile to what has been traditionally called "metaphysics." By "metaphysics" I mean roughly the kind of largely speculative thinking, not much governed by empirical or mathematical methods, that historically has been devoted to questions about what things the universe does or could contain. Since G.E. Moore (1873–1958) and Bertrand Russell (1972–1970), and through the heydays of Logical Positivism and Oxford "ordinary language" philosophy, metaphysics was regarded with suspicion or hostility in both Britain and the United States. Largely through work on the *Sophist*, these same attitudes found expression in philosophically oriented work on Plato. Antimetaphysical attitudes are much weaker now among Anglo-American philosophers than they were a couple of decades ago, but they are part of why so much work has been focused on the *Sophist*.

It ought to seem surprising that antimetaphysical attitudes should ever have had anything to do with Plato (c. 428–347). According to an age-old account, Plato was the original metaphysician, for instance the first to speak for the existence of nonphysical objects, which he frequently called "Forms" (*eide*), the first to argue for the existence of an immortal human soul, and one of the first to minimize the value of sense-experience as a source of information about how things really are. These are not good credentials for an opponent of metaphysics.

The *Sophist*, however, has been read differently. On one interpretation it does not even mention Forms, and although it uses the term *eidos* it does not on this interpretation use it to mean the "Forms" of Plato's metaphysical doctrine. It also contains passages that can be regarded as implied criticism of that doctrine as it is expounded in such earlier works as the *Phaedo* and the *Republic*. For instance, the *Sophist* speaks in seemingly disparaging tones of the "friends of the Forms" (248a).[1] For this and other reasons, many twentieth-century scholars have taken the *Sophist*, along with the *Theaetetus*, the *Parmenides*, and some other works, to express Plato's criticism of at least some (though not necessarily all) of his earlier metaphysical views.

A second reason for special modern interest in the *Sophist* is that, like much modern philosophy, the work shows interest in elucidating linguistic expressions, particularly some expressions that are central to logic. In the first place, the chief aim of the dialogue is to show that it is possible to hold a false belief, and hence that it is possible for someone—notably, a "Sophist"—to engender false beliefs in other people. Along the way the dialogue tries to explicate the expression "that which is not," because believing falsely is equated with "believing that which is not." The dialogue also examines other terms, including "not," "is" or "to be," "same," and "different." In the second place, Plato treats belief as the holding of a certain attitude toward a statement or sentence.[2] Thus he regards believing that Theaetetus is sitting as the adopting of a certain attitude of belief toward the statement, "Theaetetus is sitting." Plato mentions that Sophists create "images" (239c*sqq*.). This turns out to mean, not anything to do with pictures or other nonlinguistic representations, but the idea that Sophists cause people to hold false beliefs, that is, to believe false statements (240c–d). The understanding of how statements can be false thus becomes a central part of Plato's project. Since modern philosophy has been intensely preoccupied with issues concerning language, these two features of the *Sophist* were bound to call forth a sympathetic response.

The third reason it holds special interest recently is that the *Sophist* investigates a philosophical point reminiscent of one that was prominent in early twentieth-century philosophy, and seemed to many to be one of its notable successes. In 1905 Russell published his article "On Denoting."[3] In it he claimed to show how the notion of *nonexistence* could be expressed without the paradox that had often appeared to afflict it. His

---

1. The quotations from the *Sophist* used in this Introduction differ in certain details from what is given in the translation itself. The reason is that in the former I am giving my own interpretation, whereas in the translation I am trying, to the extent feasible, to leave interpretative questions open for the reader to answer.

2. Rather than "statement" it would sometimes be better to say "sentence" and at other times it would be better to say "proposition." For present purposes the differences do not matter much. The Greek word that Plato mostly uses is *logos*, which is broader than any of the aforementioned terms (see n. 29).

3. Russell 1905.

answer to the problem seemed to provide a lesson in how explaining a bit of language could unravel a metaphysical tangle. The problem arose because, for example, when one says "Pegasus does not exist," one seems to indicate that one is talking about a certain thing, Pegasus, and yet at the same time to say that it is not there to be talked about. Russell tried to show how this appearance of paradoxical conflict could be eliminated.

The *Sophist* mainly deals with a problem that looks much the same as Russell's. At 236ff., Plato expounds a difficulty concerning "that which is not" (*to me on*). He attributes the discovery of it to the earlier philosopher Parmenides (who died probably not long after 450 B.C.). His contention was that we cannot speak or think of that which is not. Nonetheless, Plato emphasizes, certain things that we say and think do indeed seem to require us to use the phrase "that which is not"—including even our own effort to say that we cannot speak or think of that which is not (238d–239b)!

Parmenides' difficulty seems related to Russell's problem about nonexistence. For example the statement, "That which is not cannot be spoken of," seems paradoxical in a way that is reminiscent of "Pegasus does not exist." The resemblance appears especially strong if "nonbeing" and "nonexistence" amount to the same thing. In that case we have the two statements, "Pegasus does not exist" and "That which is not cannot be spoken of," both of which look as though they single something out to talk about, but at the same time say that it is not there to be talked about. The two statements are not exactly parallel (the latter, unlike the former, tries to say explicitly that its alleged subject matter cannot be spoken of). Still, both appear to be caught up in much the same difficulty, which is roughly that of trying to speak about something that is, by hypothesis, not there at all.

It has been disputed whether the two problems are the same (cf. *infra*, pp. xx, xxviii), and whether "nonbeing" really is tantamount to "nonexistence." Nevertheless the resemblance between them makes clear why many twentieth-century interpreters of Plato have found the *Sophist* especially congenial food for philosophical and historical thought. Its problem of nonbeing, taken along with its possibly antimetaphysical and obvious linguistically oriented thinking, fits well with modern preoccupations.

## 2. Plato and the Sophists

Plato wrote the *Sophist*, it is generally agreed, after he had formulated his overall doctrine in the *Phaedo*, the *Republic*, and the *Symposium*. Scholars disagree, however, about what position on those doctrines the *Sophist* espouses. Traditionally Plato's doctrine was thought to have held constant throughout his life, each work simply laying out a different part of it. In the twentieth century, however, a developmentalist account of his thought has arisen to compete with the traditional unitarian one. Developmentalists typically believe that after he formulated his major views—the ones for which he has historically been known—he began in works like the *Theaetetus*, the *Parmenides*, and the *Sophist* to examine critically and perhaps even to reject his earlier thinking.

Even if this developmentalist story is correct, some important ideas in the *Sophist* are the same as ones that we find in much earlier works. One concerns Plato's attitude toward the people called "sophists." The sophists, as modern scholarship has made plain, were a varied group of teachers who appeared in Greek cities, especially Athens, during the second half of the fifth century B.C. Some of Plato's works give the impression that all sophists advocated the same ideas, and that he regarded them as all equally pernicious. In fact, he seems to have acknowledged significant differences among them. On the other hand, he does treat them as alike in one very important respect: they are not philosophers, and they do not make their main aim the pursuit of knowledge as he understands that term. For Plato, a philosopher aims to know what is objectively true about objectively real entities. At least in the period of the *Republic*, Plato believes that this excludes statements about sensible, physical objects, and that it necessarily involves the nonsensible, nonphysical things that he calls Forms.[4] Even more important than the Forms, however, is his thought that the philosopher strives for knowledge about what is in some strong sense objective and holds independently of what any particular person believes.

Sophists as such, in Plato's view, do not strive for this knowledge. He stresses this point from his early works right up through the *Sophist*. In the *Apology of Socrates* he portrays Socrates as differentiating himself sharply from sophists by his attempt to gain genuine knowledge. In the *Gorgias* and the *Euthydemus*, and also in the *Republic*, he criticizes the willingness of sophists like Gorgias (c. 483–376) to speak and argue for any side of a question. The *Theaetetus* speaks against the relativism of the sophist, Protagoras, according to which what any person believes is true for him, and also against an attempt—a precursor of the one in the

---

4. This statement represents the traditional and, I think, essentially correct interpretation of Plato, which some recent scholars oppose. The statement must, however, be carefully interpreted (see White (1989)).

*Sophist*—to show that false belief is impossible (187a–200c). Clearly one aim of the *Theaetetus* is to defend the idea that there are objective facts in the world that we can be right or wrong about. The *Sophist* pursues this same program. Plato says that a sophist is a deceiver, who causes people to hold false beliefs and prides himself on making people believe whatever he wants (232a–233d). In an ironic aside, Plato contrasts this activity with that of a person who cleanses people of a mistaken belief in their own wisdom (230a–231b, esp. 231a).

As Plato presents things, the thought that a sophist implants false beliefs is the motivation for the whole discussion of nonbeing that begins in 236d. To the charge that they produce false beliefs, the sophists reply that there is no such thing. Believing falsely is believing "that which is not," they say, and there can be no thought or talk about such a thing (237a, e, 238c). This reply stimulates Plato to take up the notion of nonbeing. Nonbeing, that is, is discussed not simply for its own sake, but because treating it is required, Plato thinks, to show that false beliefs are possible, and thus that sophists can cause them. Plato is of course eager to show, against Parmenides, that nonbeing can indeed be spoken and thought about. The issue does not arise, however, as an isolated problem in Parmenides' metaphysics or Plato's own. Instead it is part of a general intellectual discussion, which bears both on his own views about the possibility of objective knowledge, and on sophistic positions that are widely influential in his milieu.

In addition to the problem about nonbeing, the *Sophist* discusses another matter pertaining to what a sophist is and does. It is raised by the part of his general procedure of "dialectic," the so-called "Method of Division," which he uses before 232a to generate several definitions of the sophist. One set of problems about Division concerns how the Method is supposed to work. For example, does it aim to *demonstrate* that a particular definition is correct, or merely to formulate definitions whose correctness is to be assessed by some other means? Also, what should we make of the fact that Plato presents several applications of the Method, which yield several definitions, these being summed up in 231d–e before the treatment of nonbeing starts. Does he think that one and the same notion, or alternatively the same type or property, can be defined in different ways? Or does he think that there are different kinds of sophist? Does be believe, as 268c–d appears to indicate, that his final definition is the only correct one?

Unfortunately the *Sophist* does not answer these questions, nor explain the Method of Division itself. Plato uses the Method in other dialogues, such as the *Phaedrus* and the *Philebus*, and even makes a few explanatory remarks about it there. Nowhere, however, does he present a full account of it. Certainly the examples of its application that he presents do not suffice. He must have thought about these questions. The *Sophist*, however, does not try to make us understand the Method very deeply. The series of divisions and definitions sounds whimsical, and appears designed to presuppose rather than to supply an understanding of the Method. It also allows him to make miscellaneous comments, mostly uncomplimentary, about sophists' behavior.

The part of the dialogue until 232a, therefore, seems best interpreted as a way of presenting the general intellectual motivation for the more technical investigation of "that which is not." This is not at all to say that the first part is unimportant. It shows what Plato thought was at stake in discussing nonbeing. It makes plain, largely through illustrations, why he believed that vindicating false belief and the intelligibility of nonbeing was an important project for thinking people. If no one can say or believe anything false, he held, then the idea of objective reality and objective knowledge would be subverted. There would then be no grounds for principled objection to what he thought was the crudely self-serving and frivolously manipulative behavior that the preliminary definitions of the sophist are meant to highlight. Without the broad motivation that these definitions bring out, the investigation of "that which is not" would be a merely academic exercise. With it, though, they seemed intellectually inescapable.

## 3. The *Sophist* and Plato's Doctrine of Forms

In 232a–236e Plato broaches the idea that a sophist teaches people how to contradict others, that he creates appearances, and that he implants false beliefs. At 237a he introduces Parmenides and shows how a sophist can invoke him to testify that false belief is after all impossible. After some expansion of the Parmenidean line of argument, Plato says at 241d that false belief and false statement can be shown possible only if we

> insist by brute force both that *that which is not* somehow is, and then again that *that which is* somehow is not.

The attempt to do this is declared successful at 258c–259e. Then, in 260a–264b, he goes on to show how false statement and false belief can occur.

A major portion of 232a–264b is taken up, however, not with the actual discussion of "that which is not" and false statement, but, in 242d–255e, with some stage setting for that discussion. The stage setting, though, is far from being merely ornamental. First, it purports to tell us about necessary conditions for our being able to state anything at all, namely, the "weaving together of forms" (*symploke eidon*, 259e). Second, it contains material that seems to bear on Plato's thinking about Forms in the *Phaedo* and the *Republic*. Scholars have debated whether this material is consistent with that thinking, or, as Developmentalists contend, revises it.

Serious treatment of this second point is out of place here, because it would require us to range far beyond the *Sophist*. Still, three of the main issues should be mentioned. First, the *Sophist* raises many questions about interrelationships among what it calls "forms." (I conform to the usual convention: uppercase "Forms" when it is clear that we are dealing with the Forms of the *Phaedo* and *Republic*, and lowercase "forms" when it is not clear.)[5] Some parts of the *Phaedo* make it sound as if there is little or nothing to say about any such interrelations (78c–e, 80a–b). Although the *Republic* seems to allude to these interrelations (509d–511e), scholars sometimes maintain that Plato had little interest in them and little conceptual apparatus for investigating them until later works, particularly those where the Method of Division appears.

Second, the *Sophist* is sometimes read as explaining, as if it were a new discovery, a distinction between two ways of taking statements of the form, "A is B," as equivalent to "A is identical with B" (for example, "The morning star is the evening star") or to "A is predicatively B" or "A possesses the attribute of being B" (for example, "Socrates is wise"). This distinction between identifying and predicative statements, some scholars hold, enables Plato to correct a mistake in his earlier doctrine of Forms. On this interpretation he had previously thought of the Form of F (the Form of Large, for instance) as itself somehow an ideally F thing (in this case, an ideally large thing). This is the origin, it is said, of his notion that Forms are paradigms of which sensible objects are deficient copies (e.g., *Rep.* 484c, 595a–597e), which is based on a confusion of the identifying and predicative uses of "A is B" statements. Plato supposedly took "The large is large" to be trivially true—as it in fact is in the identifying sense of "Large(ness) is identical with Large(ness)"—but he confused this with the predicative statement, "Large(ness) is predicatively (a) large (thing),"

---

5. My own belief is that the forms of the *Sophist* are the Forms of the *Phaedo*, but nothing that I say here will depend on that contention. On issues affecting the translation of *eidos* and *idea*, see n. 26.

and so fell into thinking that the Form of Large must be a large thing, a thing with extensive dimensions. In the *Sophist*, this interpretation concludes, he freed himself from this confusion, and so also from the mistaken idea that the Form of Large is a large thing.

Third, the *Sophist* evidently maintains that "that which is" includes both that which changes and that which rests (249c–d). Many developmentalists hold that this, too, represents a change of view, since Plato earlier seems to hold that "being" can be applied only to Forms whereas sensible objects merely "become" (*Rep.* 485b, 508d, 526e).

Perhaps the *Sophist* does revise Plato's earlier views in these respects, and perhaps it does not. His coy reference in 248a to the "friends of the Forms"—whose view that "being" and "becoming" exclude each other is rejected—seems to hint at self-criticism but falls short of proving it conclusively. Perhaps the views expressed in the *Sophist* can be squared with the ones in earlier works. At all events, revisions of previous thinking are not on the official agenda of the dialogue, and can be left aside here.

## 4. Stage-Setting: The Interweaving of Forms

The weaving together of forms, Plato holds (259e), is what makes it possible for us to say anything. That is the upshot of the elaborate passage, in 242d–255e, which prepares for his account of false statement. The account itself involves saying such things as "Change is different (sc., from difference)" (265c), "Change is different (sc., from being)" (265d), "Change is (sc., a being)" (256d), "Being is different (sc., from other things)" (257a), and the like. For it to be possible to say these things, Plato maintains, the interweaving of forms must occur, or, he also holds, forms must be capable of "associating" (*koinonein*) with each other (251d–e, 254c). "Association" involves the sorts of statements just given. He might mean that every statement describes such an associative relationship (as each of these examples seems to). Or he might mean that the existence of a network of interweaving among forms is a background condition required for any statement to be meaningful, even if many statements do not individually describe or express associations. The latter seems more likely. The statement "Theaetetus sits" would accordingly not itself report an association of one form with another, but its meaning would be made possible by the fact that, for instance, the form, sitting, is different from such forms as the form, standing.

Plato expects the thesis that forms can associate to meet resistance.

Most of 242d–255e tries to overcome that resistance, which arises from several sources. He starts by focusing on the notion of being or "that which is." Against people who maintain that "that which is not" is paradoxical he replies that "that which is" is, unbeknownst to many, equally paradoxical (242b–243d). First he argues that explaining "is" presents difficulty both for those who (like Parmenides) say that "that which is" is only one thing, and also for those who say that it is only two things (243d–245e). The same difficulty can be seen, he then says, by examining the dispute between "Giants" and "Gods." Giants are those who say that only what is tangible "is." Gods are those who contend that sensible things are merely "becoming," and that only such things as souls and the virtues really "are" (245e–246d). A complex train of reasoning concludes that *both* things that change *and* things that rest "are" (249d), and that when we say that both change and rest "are," we indicate that "that which is" is a third thing alongside them (249d–250c). The problem is that this third thing, "that which is," by its own nature does not either rest or change (250c6–7). But surely, he says, what does not change must rest and what does not rest must change. So how can "that which is" lie outside of both of these (250c–d)? Therefore being raises, he says, problems just as severe as nonbeing (250d–251a).

The problems about "that which is" and "that which is not" are both to be met, Plato thinks, through the realization that forms can "associate" with each other. (But not every form can associate with every other; some—in particular, contraries—exclude each other; see 252d–e.) Association makes possible the commonsensically obvious fact that one and the same thing can be "called by many names" (251a–b). This idea is the basis of Plato's explanation of how, Parmenides notwithstanding, "that which is not" can also "be," and "that which is" can also "not be." Because "that which is not" can also "be," Plato will maintain, we can without contradiction allow that a false statement states "that which is not." A "that which is not" that at the same time "is," he thinks, can be thought of and spoken of. What makes this possible is the fact that "that which is" and "that which is not" can in fact associate or blend with each other. The reason why he undertakes to explain the workings of association in general is merely to show how this particular association, of "that which is" and "that which is not," is possible.

The interweaving of forms offers essentially the same response to the problems of both being and nonbeing that make him say that both notions are equally problematic. In both cases it is necessary to hold that a form can have certain features that it does not have simply "by its own nature," that is, by virtue of being the particular form that it is.[6] The first element of the parallel is this: "that which is" does not, simply by virtue of being "that which is," either change or rest (250c). Part of what this means is that from the fact that something "is," it *follows neither* that it rests *nor* that it changes. This is no paradox, though, because both things that change and things that rest can both "be," and a thing that "is" can either rest or change (248c–d, 251d). The second element is this: although "that which is not" does not by its own nature "be," nonetheless it can "be" by virtue of partaking in "being." A thing about which one can say that it "is not" can be said also to "be," Plato maintains, even though from the fact that it "is not," it certainly does not *follow* that it "is." Thus far the two treatments are parallel: they both depend on the fact that certain relations hold between distinct forms. These relations enable forms to have features distinct from and not directly due to their own natures.

Beyond this point, though, the parallel ends. There is no great difficulty if change and rest partake in being. But the partaking of nonbeing in being, Plato indicates, is much more problematical. For nonbeing and being have the look of contraries, and so they seem to exclude each other— to refuse to "blend," just as change and rest refuse to (252d–e). This is the main issue that Plato has to tackle when the stage-setting is over in 255e and he must focus directly on "that which is not." We shall take the issue up after doing some stage-setting of our own.

## 5. The Problem of Falsehood in Dialogues before the *Sophist*

The problem about falsehood with which the *Sophist* deals is raised briefly in works preceding it. Plato mentions the issue in the *Euthydemus* and the *Cratylus*, but does not offer a solution. In those works, as in the *Sophist*, the problem is generated by the notion of "that which is not." In *Theaetetus* 188c–189b, too, a very similar difficulty is raised but left without an answer.

Problems about nonbeing also crop up briefly in the *Republic*, in a passage concerned with the distinction between knowledge (*episteme*) and belief or opinion (*doxa*). Something that "is not" could not be known, Plato says (476e–477a). Then he also denies that one could "believe that which is not," and claims that that would be equivalent to "believing nothing"

6. See 255e and also Lee 1972 and Meinwald 1991.

(478b–c). "That which is not," he maintains, is what "ignorance" (*agnoia*) deals with (477a, 478c). Belief, he concludes, has to do with what is "between" that which "is" and that which "is not" (477a, 478d), or what "simultaneously is and is not" (478d). His example of the latter is a sensible object that appears, from different viewpoints, both beautiful and ugly, or both light and heavy (479a–d). Evidently being and nonbeing here amount to "being F" and "being the contrary of F."[7] It is noteworthy, however, that Plato does not here engage in any discussion of the notion of falsity or false belief.[8]

However things may be in the *Republic*, the *Theaetetus* does make a sustained attack on a problem about false belief. However, only a small part of that examination, namely, the brief and inconclusive discussion in 188c–189d, has to do with nonbeing and the issues raised in the *Sophist*. The rest of the passage on falsity, 187a–200c, confronts the possibility of false belief with a quite different problem, which the *Sophist* never so much as hints at. It arises from taking a false belief to be about something that the believer in some sense has in mind (or that he "knows," Plato often says). The question then is how, if he genuinely has that thing in mind (or knows it), he can possibly make a mistake about it. In particular, Plato wonders how the believer can confuse the thing he has in mind with something else. Solving the problem plainly involves maintaining that a person can have an object in mind, in the sense necessary for having a belief that is about it in the relevant way, without having the object in mind so completely, so to speak, that he cannot make any mistakes about it and cannot mistakenly identify it with anything else. In the *Theaetetus* Plato does not develop an account of belief about an object that would allow him to maintain this. Accordingly he ends the discussion there without a solution.

The *Sophist* leaves this particular problem about false belief in the same unsolved state. It shows no awareness of any need to explain how there can be a false belief about a particular thing. To believe, Plato there says, is simply to accept a certain statement (263e–264a), and a statement is about a thing if a term in the sentence is a "name" of the thing (263a, 262a). Perhaps he thinks that this is all it takes for a thing to be an object of a false belief. If so, however, he does not explain why the *Theaetetus* was

---

7. The following is important: from the fact that a sensible simultaneously appears both F and the contrary of F, Plato here takes himself to be entitled to infer that it in some sense *is* both F and the contrary of F.

8. For a hypothesis about why see Denyer 1991, Ch. 4.

wrong to maintain that a believer who genuinely has something in mind cannot hold a false belief about it. Instead the *Sophist* concentrates exclusively on the problem about nonbeing.

## 6. The Equation of False Stating with Stating That Which Is Not

Starting at *Sophist* 236d, Plato lays out the argument against the possibility of falsehood. A false belief is a belief in a certain kind of statement, one that states something false. Stating falsely, the argument says, is the same as "stating that which is not." Harking back to Parmenides, the argument then contends that "that which is not" cannot be spoken or thought of. The conclusion is that someone who tries to say "that which is not" is stating nothing.

We can describe the problem at a number of different levels. At a quite abstract one, the difficulty arises because a condition alleged to be required for making a false statement, namely "stating that which is not," allegedly turns out to entail that a statement has not been made at all. The solution to the problem is simply to take care that, when one explains the conditions for the falsity and the conditions for the making of a statement, the satisfaction of the former not turn out to entail a failure to satisfy the latter.

Sometimes it is maintained that Plato's problem arose because he tacitly accepted a view of the meaning of statements that made it difficult for him to do this. On this interpretation, he thought that for a statement to be meaningful was for it to correspond to a certain entity, but at the same time fell into thinking, too, that the truth of the sentence consisted in its correspondence to the very same entity. For example, philosophers have sometimes thought both that the meaning of a statement is a "fact" that it expresses, and that its truth consists in corresponding to the same fact. But then it seems that if the sentence is false, like "Theaetetus flies," then there is no such fact for it to correspond to, no such fact, that is, as the fact that Theaetetus flies. Therefore, it appears, there is likewise no fact for it to express in order to be meaningful. So a false statement turns out necessarily to be meaningless. If Plato tacitly thought along these lines, his problem about false statement could arise this way.[9]

There will be more comments to make about this interpretation when we consider Plato's treatment of falsity in 261c–263d (see p. xxviii). For

9. For a discussion of the idea that Plato's problem of false statement arose because he felt drawn to such a theory, see Owen (1970) and Denyer 1991, esp. Ch. 9.

the moment, however, note that his formulation of his problem does not give any explicit support to the interpretation. He does not talk about what it is for a whole statement to be meaningful. He does not even allude to the need for such an account.

For all that Plato's own presentation of his problem tells us, its origin is simply the Equation of false stating with "stating that which is not"— hereafter often simply "the Equation"—together with the alleged paradoxicality of the latter notion. This, without any further theory about how a statement is meaningful, yields the problem as he expounds it. It also fits with the first step toward his solution (241d with a–b). That step is simply an attempt to show that the phrase "that which is not" has an intelligible and noncontradictory interpretation. It is presented on its own, not as a part of an account of the meaning of a statement.

The Equation of false stating with "stating that which is not" seems to have become entrenched in philosophical discourse after Parmenides. It seems also to have sounded entirely natural as a piece of ordinary Greek speech. There, perhaps, "that which is not" should be implicitly taken as in effect equivalent to "that which is not the case."[10] Still, Plato could not have disarmed his problem by merely pointing out that "that which is not" here merely means, unproblematically, "that which is not the case." His opponents would simply have replied that the notion of "that which is not the case" needs to be elucidated too. The sophists, after all, had a strong motivation to reject the notion of falsehood. They would not have been likely to rest content with the uninformative platitude that falsity is not being the case, unless there was a showing that the latter notion itself was free from paradox.

## 7. The Problem about That Which Is Not and Russell's Problem about Existence

Plato accepts the Equation, then, and so he must try to show that "stating that which is not" is possible. This he does in two steps. The first step is to argue, as already noted (p. xv), that "that which is not" is an intelligible, nonselfcontradictory notion. The second step is to make clear, on this basis, what "stating that which is not" consists in, thus showing that such a thing can occur.

The first step consists in showing that "that which is not" and "that which is" can "blend" (258e–259b). This in turn involves showing at least

10. See Kahn 1966.

that "is" and "is not" are not incompatible, as Parmenides had thought they were. But Plato goes even further. We can say, he argues, that "that which is not" itself "is," and that "that which is" likewise "is not" (258c–e). He argues, in other words, that being and nonbeing can be interpreted so as not to be "contraries" (257b, 258a–b). They do not stand to each other as change and rest do. Change and rest exclude each other, he says, in the sense that nothing that is changing can be at rest, and vice versa.[11] Moreover, he maintains (and the meaning here is controversial[12]), change does not rest and rest does not change. "That which is" and "that which is not," he argues, do not stand to each other in this way.

In taking his first step Plato rejects the position that when "is not" is clearly understood it excludes "is." The Parmenidean arguments in 236d–239c insist that if something "is not" in the strict and proper sense, then nothing can be said about it at all: it is not anything (237d–e, 238b–c, 239b). The principle appears to be that "that which is not" *just means* "that which in no way is" (237b), which in turn *just means* the paradoxical idea of a thing to which no expression can correctly be applied.

The paradox here is not quite that of the descriptive phrase, "thing that no expression designates." Rather, like virtually all such Greek expressions, "that which in no way is" (*to medamos on*) carries a grammatical sign of singular number. It therefore seems to attribute "oneness" to what it designates, in contradiction to its own suggestion that what it designates has nothing to be said about it at all. The problem thus seems to hinge on a seeming conflict between trying to designate an object with an expression that both (a) employs expressions ascribing "oneness" to the object, and (b) specifies the object as incapable of having anything at all ascribed to it.

Is the problem here like Russell's, of referring to an object and then saying that it is not there to be referred to, or is it a different problem? That question does not have a clear answer. On the latter side one could argue that the difficulty really arises from tying the notion of falsehood to a self-contradictory *predicate*, "is thus-and-so and is not thus-and-so." Parmenides would be contending, in effect, that calling a statement false would be roughly comparable to trying to conceive the notion of being

---

11. The formulation of this point has to be handled carefully. As Plato knows (*Rep.* 436d–e), a thing can be at rest in one respect and in motion in another.

12. Because it seems to involve him in the view that the Form of F (motion, rest) is predicatively F (in motion, at rest)—a view that some interpreters think he abandoned in his later works (cf. pp. xiii–xiv).

both square and not square. That would seem to be a conceptual paradox, but not the Russellian one about trying to talk about what is not there to be talked about.[13] On the other hand, Plato formulates his problem in terms of a singular term, "that which is not," which seems to try abortively, so to speak, to pick out an object but then fails to do so.[14] In that way it might seem to revolve around an attempt to try to refer to something that does not exist. That would assimilate it to Russell's sort of problem. It is not clear that there is any point in insisting on one of these two alternatives over the other (see further, p. xxviii).

## 8. That Which Is Not and That Which Is Not Concerning X

It will be useful to describe the two steps of Plato's argument a little more closely. The first involves pointing out that whereas "change is not rest," nevertheless "change 'is' (because it partakes in being)" (255e, 256c, 256a). Likewise: whereas "change is the same (because it partakes in sameness in relation to itself)," it also "is not the same (because it partakes in difference in relation to sameness)" (256a10–b4); and whereas "change is different (because it is different from difference)," it "is not different (also because it is different from difference" (256c5–9). In addition, whereas "change is being (because it partakes in being)" (256d9), it "is not being (because it is different from being)" (256d5–8). Plato generalizes thus: each genus "is" or "is being" because it "partakes in being" (256e3), and each genus also "is not being" because it "is different from being" (256e2). But being itself both "is," because it is itself (257a5), and "is not," because it "is different from the others" (257a4–6; cf. 255d12–e1). The pattern is this: a thing "is" either by partaking in being or (in the case of being itself) by being being; and a thing "is not" by being different from (and in that sense "not being") something else. Plato thus ends up identifying, in a sense, *nonbeing* with *difference*.

As part of his description of this first step, Plato also says something that prepares the way for his second step. He introduces the notion of

---

13. In fact, this seems to be more like the problem that worried the historical Parmenides.
14. Notice that instead of the singular term "that which is not" Plato could have formulated his paradox in terms of the grammatical *predicate* "is not (in any way)." Its verb carries (in Greek as in English) a sign of singular number and thus could be taken in effect as tantamount to "is one and is neither one nor anything else." Perhaps one should take the fact that he did not do this as a reason to regard his problem as closer to Russell's than it might be.

*"being in the case of (or concerning, or about)"* something. Roughly, A "is concerning" B just in case A applies to B. Thus, "that which is not," he says, "is concerning change, and over all the other kinds" (256d11–12). This is because difference makes each kind different from "that which is," and difference is identified with "that which is not." The important point here is that difference, *alias* "that which is not," is said to "be" on the strength of the fact that it *applies to* the other kinds. To generalize: one way in which a feature of form can "be" is to be applicable to something.[15]

Plato uses this idea in the second step, his actual account of false statement, as follows. The simplest kind of statement, he says, such as "(A) man learns" or "Theaetetus sits" (262a, 263a), consists of a "name" and a "verb." The name "signifies a thing that performs an action" (262a). That thing is what the statement is "of" (262e–263a). A true statement, like "Theaetetus sits," "says those which are, that (or, as) they are concerning" Theaetetus (263b). A false statement like "Theaetetus flies," on the other hand, "says things different from those that are," or, in other words, it says "those which are not, that they are (or, as being) concerning" Theaetetus. For, Plato says, "many beings are concerning [Theaetetus], and many are not" (263b). A false statement, accordingly, says "that which is not," in the following sense: it says things that are different from the things that are concerning Theaetetus. In more idiomatic English, it attributes to Theaetetus characteristics different from those that are correctly attributable to him. Here as in the first step, the explanation of nonbeing again involves difference. However, instead of "that which is" we now have "that which is concerning X," or, as we might equally say, "that which is with respect to X." And so, likewise, "that which is not" has become "that which is not concerning X."

## 9. The Notion of Being, as a Component of the Notion of Being Concerning X

We can begin to clarify the situation by raising a question about Plato's strategy. In order to show that false statements are possible, Plato makes use of the notion of "that which is not *concerning X*." In that case, however, why does he need to raise problems about the seemingly different notion of "that which is not" taken by itself, without the "concerning X" part? Why could he not have ignored this notion—which, after all, is the notion

---

15. This is not to say that this is the only way in which a feature can be said to "be."

that raises all the fuss from 236 on? He could simply have said that "Theaetetus flies" says "that which is not concerning Theaetetus." Then he could have explained this (if explanation was necessary) by claiming that it says something concerning Theaetetus that is different from things that are concerning him. There would have been no need to discuss any problems about "that which is not." The *Sophist* could then have been very much shorter.

To attack this question one must raise a broader question about Plato's use of "is" and "is not." This will make it possible to see why Plato felt that, in order to show that "that which is not concerning X" is an intelligible notion, he had also to show the same for "that which is not" *simpliciter.*

Plato has, first, what I would call an "uncomplemented" use of the expressions "is" and "is not."[16] It is exemplified by sentences like "Change is" and "Change is not," where the verb is followed by no complement. Second, there is also a "complemented" use, as in "Change is the same (as itself)," "Rest is not being" and, in addition, "Flying is not concerning Theaetetus." Here the verb "is" is followed by a complement.

Modern students of the *Sophist* have been much interested in Plato's "uncomplemented" use of "is." One of the reasons is their simultaneous interest in Russell's work on existence. They have noticed that uncomplemented uses of "is" can easily seem equivalent to "exist." Thus, "Change is" might seem to mean "Change exists." If so, Plato's problem about nonbeing might turn out to be the same as Russell's about nonexistence (cf. pp. viii and xix). Some have thought that Plato actually distinguishes two senses of "is," one meaning "exists" and the other functioning as a copula.[17]

But if Plato thinks that complemented "is" and uncomplemented "is" express different senses, and that the same holds of complemented "is not" and uncomplemented "is not," then his procedure in the *Sophist* becomes difficult to make sense of. For in that case there would be no apparent reason why understanding "is not concerning X," which Plato

---

16. This is not the same distinction as the one marked by Plato at 255c between "things that are said by themselves" and "things said in relation to other things." See Frede 1967 and Owen (1970). I prefer the terms "uncomplemented" and "complemented" to Owen's "complete" and "incomplete," respectively, because his terms suggests that there are two syntactically different terms involved (see his 1957 and 1970). In my view he does not look at the matter in that way (indeed, it is anachronistic to ascribe to him the notion of "syntax" that is implied therein).

17. See Ackrill (1957).

uses to explain falsehood, should require vindicating the other expression "is not."

His procedure makes much better sense on the assumption that he takes the meaning of "is" and "is not" to be the same in both complemented and uncomplemented uses. We could then suppose that, as he sees things, the notion expressed by the uncomplemented use, in both the affirmative and the negative case, is a *component* in the meaning of the complemented use. "A is not B," for example, *contains* the notion expressed by "is not" in "A is not." For that reason, to defend the notion expressed by the complemented use in the phrase "is not concerning Theaetetus," we must also defend the notion expressed by the uncomplemented use which is a component of it.

It turns out that Plato's earlier works provide us with a way of understanding why he held this view. For there is a parallel, which has not been noticed, between his thinking about being and nonbeing in the *Sophist*, on the one hand, and, on the other hand, his earlier ideas about the application of predicates to Forms and sensible objects. The parallel is independent of whether the *Sophist* retains the doctrine of Forms as Plato had previously formulated it.

According to works in the period of the *Phaedo* and the *Republic*, there is a special relationship between uncomplemented and complemented uses of predicates of a wide variety, including "large," "hard," "heavy," "good," "equal," and many others. "Heavy" is a good example. Circumstances determine which things are normally called heavy. One and the same thing may acceptably be called heavy on some occasions and light on others. Which is acceptable usually depends on such circumstances as which other things have recently been held and hefted. One judges the baby heavy when one has just been holding a dish, but light after one has been lugging a toddler.

Sometimes people conclude from this fact that "heavy" really means the same as the relational "heavy*er than*" something—heavier than the spoon, or than things that one has recently held, or than the average thing that one has held, or the like. This idea runs into two sorts of difficulty. One is that of specifying what exactly the baby is, on this view, being said to be heavier than. All possibilities that have been suggested seem to run into crippling objections.[18] The other difficulty is this: *insofar as* our

18. See esp. John Wallace 1972.

introspection is a reliable indicator of what we mean,[19] it turns out that when we say the baby is heavy, normally we do not mean to say that it is heav*ier than* anything at all. Rather what we mean, reasonably or not, is that he is heavy, just plain *heavy*. Circumstances, including comparisons that we can make, play an essential role in determining the acceptability of what we say. They do not enter, however, into the *meaning* that we actually intend by it—if, that is, that meaning is what introspection takes it to be.

In Plato's view the meaning of "heavy" does not involve reference to a comparison, nor to anything else about the circumstances in which, or the perspective from which, the term is applied. The same point holds for "good," "beautiful," "equal," and the other terms that he focuses on. To grasp the meaning of "heavy" is to grasp the notion of something that is heavy *apart from* comparison and perspective.

Plato thinks that understanding such terms involves knowledge of a Form, not just experience of sensibles to which we try to apply the notion. He conceives of the Forms as cognizable independently of perspective and circumstances, particularly circumstances in which a thing might appear as non-F or the contrary of F. That inevitably happens when one apprehends sensible instances of F (*Phdo.* 74b–c, *Rep.* 479a–c), because sensibles are embedded in space and time, and thus can always be viewed from various perspectives that engender contrary appearances.[20] Rather he thinks that knowing the Form involves conceiving the notion (problematical as it obviously is in at least some cases) of a thing's being F apart from, without reference to, circumstances and perspectives.[21]

---

19. Of course many twentieth century philosophers—most famously, Wittgenstein—deny that it is.

20. See White (1989) and (1992). Plato's idea about Forms is not that the Form of F is the notion of something that is F from all sensible perspectives or in all physical circumstances. The idea of a pair of things that looks equal from all angles, for example, would be absurd, at least if the things are thought of as embedded in space, given that one could always look at them in such a way that one was closer than the other, and so would in the relevant way appear larger.

21. See also *Symp.* 211a–b. I am not maintaining that this idea is clear or fully defensible, though I think it contains something of philosophical value. (It certainly runs against a strong tendency in recent philosophy to try—though unsuccessfully—to define positive terms like "heavy" in terms of comparative terms like "heavier." Plato's tendency is the reverse: to think of "heavier" as composed of the notion of "heavy" combined with a notion of degree or "more/less" (this fact emerges in the fragments of his lecture, *De Bono*).

Nonetheless Plato thinks that in our ordinary thinking we do try to apply these very notions to sensible objects. He never indicates that instead of sometimes calling certain sensible things "hard," we should instead always call them hard*er than* something or other. It would come a bit closer to say that we call such things "*hard, compared to* this or that," or "hard, in this or that way." He speaks for instance of the girl whom we are inclined to call "beautiful" when we compare her to a pot, even though we are equally strongly inclined to call her "not beautiful" when we compare her to a goddess. We take a term whose meaning we understand as perspective- and circumstance-independent, and we apply it to sensible things, to which (as we easily recognize when we think about favorable cases, as at *Rep.* 523a–525c) the term applies only from certain perspectives and in certain circumstances.[22] When we become aware of this state of affairs, we then recognize that a sensible object is in a sense not strictly *hard*, for example, but rather that it—in Plato's jargon—"partakes of" or "participates in" hardness. But that is not what we *mean* when we call it "hard." Nor does it accurately report the nature of our sensory experience, even when we are aware of the variability of contexts of comparison, and even after we are aware of the existence of the Form. That experience, though we recognize that it is embedded in a context of comparison, can still be as of a thing that is hard.[23]

Quite apart from whether the *Sophist* accepts all of Plato's earlier doctrine about Forms, this is how the notion of being ought to be construed here. A thing, sensible or not, can be said to "be such-and-such." It can

22. For the case of the girl see *Hipp. Mai.* 289a–c. Many of Plato's views are mysterious if this point is ignored, but they come into focus once it is appreciated. First, this is one reason why Plato thinks that the expressions that we apply to sensibles are "really" the "names" of Forms (*Phdo.* 102b–c, 103b–c). Second, it is part of the reason why he says that sensibles "fall short" of being just like Forms (*Phdo.* 74–75), and also why he thinks of sensibles as "images" of Forms (*Rep.* 495–97). Notice especially how important it is to his thinking in the last-mentioned passage that images must be created from a particular *perspective*, whereas what a thing "really is" is not. (In addition, it helps explain why he thinks of the cognition of Forms as a kind of mental "seeing"—e.g., *Rep.* 475e, 500c, 511, and *Symp.* 210e—since the notions that we consider when we have knowledge of a Form are precisely the ones that we take in, so to speak, through our senses.)

23. Recognizing that the experience is conditional on context, that is, does not change what we take as the *content* of the experience (or the judgment that we base on it), which makes no reference to the context *even after the recognition has taken place*. An analogy: when one looks at two equal sticks that are at different distances from one's eyes, one is aware of the situation and realizes that they are equal, *but* nevertheless they still, in a perfectly clear way, *look unequal* (*Phdo.* 74b–c).

also be said simply to "be," *apart from* any reference to any "such-and-such"—whether the "such-and-such" is a predicate or a phrase like "concerning Theaetetus." "Being" in this sense should be thought of as standing to "being such-and-such" in approximately the same way as the (in Plato's view) nonrelational notion expressed by "heavy" stands to the idea expressed by "heavy, compared to X."[24] That is, they are the very same notion. The only difference is that in the latter case the notion of being is being used within a certain context, which is acknowledged by the "such-and-such" as an addendum to the predicate. The notion expressed by "is" is thus, as already indicated (p. xxiv), a component in the meaning expressed by "is such-and-such."

This, then, is the reason why Plato needs to defend the uncomplemented use of "is" in order to be secure in the use of "is concerning X." To use the latter is to use the former as a part of it, and thus the latter cannot be understood unless the former is too.[25] Moreover because both uses express the same meaning, in his view, both must be given the same explanation.[26]

## 10. The Restricted Aim of the *Sophist*

Does "is" in Plato's uncomplemented use express a notion of existence? Obviously not, it might seem. Matters are not, however, quite so simple. Three points should be borne in mind. First, since Frege and Russell quite a lot of philosophers have tended to think that a notion of existence must be something that is expressed by an existential quantifier, "there is an object such that . . .," or else by a predicate applied to possible objects saying that they are actual (and not only possible). Plato's usage does not easily fit either of those specifications, but the specifications may be too narrow to catch the full range of the concept. Second, he shows no interest in how to say that Pegasus did not exist or that unicorns do not, nor in whether the idea of a nonexistent Pegasus should be banished as thor-

---

24. Cf. Brown 1986. Plato also suggests that "being" is equivalent to "having power, sc., to do or suffer something" (247d, 248d). Whether he accepts it as a final definition is not clear. He might, for example, take it to be only a sufficient but not a necessary condition.

25. Plato would thus in effect be presupposing a natural enough principle of compositionality. A principle of this sort is discussed in *Tht.* 200ff.

26. To a modern philosophical outlook, schooled to regard "X is" as meaning "X exists" and to regard the latter as representable by the existential quantifier, "There is an object X such that . . . X . . .," this idea can seem absurd. Perhaps it is ultimately unsound, but there is something to be said for it.

oughly as the Parmenidean "contrary of being." We have no good way of telling how he would react to these questions. Still, he might maintain that everything exists that can be said to "be" anything at all. Then Pegasus would exist and Plato would have to find a good way of saying that he is not actual. Third, if Plato's uncomplemented "is" means the same as his complemented "is," then to say that the former means "exists" we would have to accept the consequence that the notion of existence is expressed by the second word of, for example, "Socrates is wise." That would require some explanation, but I do not think it should be regarded as obviously absurd.

Another point about existence. I alluded earlier to an interpretation according to which Plato's problem arises because he took the meaning of a statement to be an entity, such as a fact, to which it corresponds. The worry was that if the statement is false (p. xviii), the entity does not exist and the statement turns out to be meaningless. His treatment of false belief in 261c–263d changes in the direction of this idea, but it does not make much of it.

At 261d–262d Plato claims that the simplest sort of statement, such as "(A) man learns," consists of a "verb," which indicates an action, and a "name," which signifies what performs the action. A string of names or verbs, though, such as "walks runs likes" or "lion stag horse," does not *say anything* (that is, it is not a *logos*, 262b). When you put a name and a verb together, however, you get an expression that "does not merely name," but "accomplishes something," that is, it "says something" (262c–d). These observations are important. They manifest the thought that "saying something," in the sense of making a statement, is different from simply naming an object. They therefore come very close to the idea that the meaningfulness of a statement consists in something besides mere association or correlation with some entity in the world. Nouns and verbs are explained as corresponding to objects, but the *logos* as a whole is not.

All the same, this distinction is not Plato's key to solving his difficulty over false statement. He does not say, for example, that the reason why a false but meaningful statement is possible is that the meaningfulness of a statement does not depend on the existence of a fact for it to report. For one thing, he never explicitly rejects the claim that a meaningful statement must correspond to something. In 262c–d he merely omits to assert it. If this were his solution to the problem, one would certainly expect him to announce it more openly.

In a sense he evades the whole issue. False stating had been equated to "stating that which is not." That idea is then reconstrued to mean that a false statement *about a thing* "states something different from those which are *concerning it*" (263b). This certainly has the *effect* of *calling off* any search that anyone might have made for an entity for the whole statement to correspond to. The focus of Plato's efforts, though, is *not* to *deny* that there is such an entity. Instead the focus is on explaining "is not concerning X" as "is different from those which are concerning X." Plato's main problem is therefore not, "How can a false statement be meaningful if no fact exists to which it corresponds?" but rather "How can a statement state that which is not?" and this then becomes "How can a statement state that which is not concerning X?"

We may wonder why the *Sophist* does not deal more directly with problems about existence, but we really should not. Its aim, after all, was not to investigate being in general. It was not even to answer all problems arising out of Parmenides' thought. It was just to show that false statement and belief are possible. Because of the Equation of stating falsely with "stating that which is not," he was forced to defend the sensicality of that phrase, under some interpretation. That in turn required an investigation of being, but only enough for the purposes at hand. So long as the possibility of *some* false statements was secure, statements about existence or nonexistence did not have to be among them.

Given Plato's specific purposes, there was indeed no reason for him to tackle all issues about nonbeing. As is often noted, he says nothing explicit about negative predications, such as "Theaetetus is not flying." Some interpreters suggest that by this sentence he meant, "Flying is different from those which are concerning Theaetetus"—the same thing as his explanation of the falsity of "Theaetetus flies" at 263b. In other words, "Theaetetus is not flying" would be explained as "'Theaetetus flies' is false"—not the normal order of explanation nowadays, but not entirely unreasonable either. Though I think it is fair to say that he would accept this equivalence, he does not explicitly formulate it. Moreover he was not obliged to explain every instance of "not," any more than he was obliged to explain every use of "to be." He does say that being needs accounting for just as urgently as nonbeing, and he tentatively offers a rough explanation of it (cf. 247e). He also makes a remark about negative particles (257b–c). He might have expanded that remark into an account of negation, at least of some kinds, but he did not do so.[27] Still, his task just was

---

27. Even here Plato does not say how to explain the statement, "Theaetetus is not wise." As often remarked, the passage might be taken to suggest that negation is attached to predicates, and it does not focus on the idea of negation as attached to whole statements (or

to show, without begging any questions against his opponents, that some statements can be false. It was not to explain the workings of being and "not" exhaustively.

## 11. Difference in the *Sophist*

After all of his stage setting is complete, Plato finally attempts in 261c–263d to explain what a false statement is. The falsity of "Theaetetus flies," he holds, consists in the fact that it says (concerning Theaetetus) something "*different* from those that are concerning him" (263b). A natural way to take the phrase "different from *those* that are" is as "different from *all the things* that are concerning him."[28] "'Theaetetus flies' is false" would then be construed as equivalent to saying that all of the characteristics that Theaetetus possesses are distinct from flying, or, in other words, Theaetetus possesses only characteristics different from flying. For Plato's immediate purposes, and given assumptions that he would naturally accept, this account would be adequate.[29]

Earlier, in 255e–257e, Plato gives a treatment of the word "not." That word, he maintains, does not indicate the *contrary* of the word that follows it. Rather, it indicates *difference*. He says that "what we call 'not beautiful' is the thing that's different from nothing other than the nature of the beautiful" (257d). This might be taken to say that "not beautiful" means "is different from beautiful" in the sense of "X has some characteristic different from beauty." This, though, would yield an inadequate account. A thing can possess a characteristic different from beauty and still be beautiful. The thing might, for instance, possess justice, which is different from beauty.

In response to this problem some have taken "different" to mean "incompatible." Under this reading Plato would be saying, in effect, that "is not beautiful" means something like "has a characteristic incompatible

---

sentences). On the other hand Plato is certainly not committed to treating "not" as an operator on predicates. Cf. Wiggins 1970.

28. See Owen (1970), p. 238. Some interpreters take it to mean, in effect, "different from *some of* the things that are concerning him." This obviously will not give an adequate construal of falsity (since each of the characteristics that he has is different from some of the things that are concerning him), and moreover it is not a natural rendering of the Greek of 263b7, *hetera ton onton*.

29. I do not mean that it is adequate by the standards that have come to be adopted in recent philosophy, especially in connection with the work of Tarski. There are many issues on this front that I shall not discuss here.

with beauty." He would also be explaining the falsity of "Theaetetus flies" by "Theaetetus is something that is *incompatible* with flying," i.e., "Theaetetus has some characteristic incompatible with flying."

This interpretation is subject to three severe difficulties. One is that in earlier passages, Plato plainly uses "different" *not* to mean "incompatible," but in its usual sense of "nonidentical." At 256a, for instance, he says that change is "different" from sameness. Obviously, though, change and sameness are not incompatible in the relevant way. A second difficulty is that by "same" (*tauton*) Plato throughout clearly means sameness or identity, and he plainly does not mean "compatibility." He links "same" and "different," though, in such a way that it seems impossible to believe that he means "identical" by the former and "incompatible" by the latter (see for example 256a–b). A third difficulty is this. Plato could not easily expect his opponents to accept an explanation of falsehood in terms of incompatibility. The incompatibility of a characteristic with flying, they would have said, just amounts to the fact that if something has that characteristic, then necessarily the thing *is not* flying, or, it is *false* that it is flying. They would then accuse Plato of simply reintroducing the notion that they were questioning. His whole investigation would be chicanery— such obvious chicanery that he could not have expected to get away with it.[30]

Suppose instead that we try to understand 255e–257d in accordance with the reading of 261c–263d described above, which seemed to give us a satisfactory account of the falsity of "Theaetetus flies," as meaning that Theaetetus possesses only characteristics different from flying. "'X is F' is false" then comes to this: "X has only characteristics different from F," or, "Every characteristic of X is different from F." Suppose that Plato takes "'X is F' is false" to be equivalent to "X is not F." As I remarked (p. xxix), Plato never states this equivalence (and does not explicitly offer to explain negative predication), but it seems a natural thing for him to accept.

Now consider his claim that "not beautiful" means "different from

---

30. Some interpreters say that Plato is not trying to explain what "is not" means, but merely to describe a condition under which a thing can "not be"—to show, for instance, that even if a thing "is not" one thing it can at the same time "be" something else. (Cf. McDowell 1982.) But this is not enough for Plato. He needs not only to say that a thing can both be (one thing) and not be (another). He is obliged to interpret the expression "is not" itself, in order to rebut his opponent's charge that by its very meaning it is self-contradictory (cf. above, p. 16). And to do this it is not enough for him to say what it does not mean (that it does not mean "contrary of being"); he must also say what it does mean.

beautiful," and take this to indicate that "is not beautiful" means "is different from beautiful." As we have seen this cannot mean "is *something different from beautiful.*" For a thing could be just, for example, and thus be something different from beautiful, while at the same time being beautiful. Rather, "X is not beautiful" should mean, in line with 261c–263d—to put it awkwardly at first—"X is *everything* different from beautiful," or in other words, "*Everything* that X is, is different from beautiful," or, in yet other words, "X has *only* characteristics different from beautiful." This is parallel to what Plato says about the falsity of "Theaetetus flies": it amounts to his having *only* characteristics different from flying. To generalize, not being F thus comes to this: having only characteristics different from F.[31]

This idea seems to be what Plato was trying to get at. Nevertheless his presentation of it is problematical, and suggests that he has not completely thought it through. For one thing, he is wrong to talk as though it *merely* involves construing "not" as signifying difference. In fact what it expresses is a far more complex notion, that of having only characteristics different from F. In effect, he leaves this notion as an unanalyzed primitive. Given its evident complexity, though, that seems undesirable.

Full explanation of the notion would have involved substantial discussion of the quantificational expressions that it involves. For "having only characteristics different from F" amounts to this: "for every characteristic, G, if X possesses G, then G is different from F." This uses the universal quantifier, "for every object, X." Plato did not try to explain or even focus attention on quantificational expressions. He therefore could not have self-consciously explained the notion of "having only characteristics different from" in terms of them.

If he had, moreover, he would have come to realize that the universal quantifier, "for every object X, . . . X . . . ," is intimately related to another quantifier, "for some object, X, . . . X . . . ," since "For every object, X, X is such-and-such," is equivalent to "There is no object, X, such that X

---

31. We need to know why Plato says at 257d that "the not beautiful is *the* thing that's different from nothing other than the beautiful." Other things besides not being beautiful are different from being beautiful. (Moreover other things besides simply being nonbeautiful are incompatible with being beautiful—another reason not to accept "incompatible" as a rendering of Plato's "different" here.) He is talking about the characteristic of having only characteristics different from beauty. *This* characteristic is *defined in terms of* difference from beauty (not *its* difference from beauty). He therefore thinks of it as *by its nature* different from beauty (cf. p. xvi and Lee 1972, Meinwald 1991), even though of course *its* being different from beauty is not the *whole* of its nature.

is not such-and-such." The "existential" quantifier, "there is an object, X, such that . . . ," is, of course, the expression that Russell used in his solution to his problem about how to express the notion of nonexistence. It is clear, though, that Plato did not push his own investigations so far as to investigate such quantificational expressions.

Plato's treatment of his problem also pulls up short at another point. He employs the notions expressed by "same" and "different" without ever trying to explain the relation between them. It is easy to see why. The natural explanation introduces the very problematical notions that he was trying to cope with. For X to be the same as Y seems to amount to its *not being* different from Y, and for X to be different from Y seems to amount to its *not being* the same as Y. One need not insist that a particular one of the two must be defined in terms of the other. However it would seem desirable to be able to explain the relation between them, and not leave it as primitive. Plato's account in the *Sophist*, however, cuts off the natural path of explanation.[32]

## 12. Conclusion

It should be emphasized once again, however, that Plato's purposes in the *Sophist* were limited. They did not extend to explaining negation, nor all notions of nonbeing, nor every sentence containing "to be" or the word "not." His aim was merely to show that falsity of statement and belief, understood as stating and believing "that which is not," could be understood in a nonparadoxical way. He did not have to push his account as far as he might have. For that reason he did not notice certain difficulties that his opponents might have exploited if they had seen them (which in all probability they did not). He did, however, clear away the immediate obstacles to the notion of false statement that they had set in his way.[33]

32. In the same way, it also cuts off the path to explaining other logical relationships that are normally expressed in terms of negation. For example, Plato never explicitly suggests a way in which the relation of "contrariety" can be explained, for example between rest and motion. That certain forms are "contrary" is taken as a brute fact. (In 257b Plato does not reject the notion of contrariety; he merely denies that it is involved in a certain use of "not.") It could be explained, it seems, in terms of his notion of difference, i.e., the notion of "having only characteristics that are different from." But that would leave the relation between "same" and "different" primitive, as I have just said.

33. As I have indicated (p. xvii), he does not in the *Sophist* deal with all of the problems about false *belief* that he presents in the *Theaetetus*. The *Sophist* is therefore more successful with the problem of false statement than it is with that of false belief, precisely because it accepts a hasty reduction of the latter problem to the former.

From our point of view the fundamental misstep in Plato's treatment of the problem is his initial equation of believing and stating falsely to believing and stating "that which is not" (cf. p. xix). That equation, taken over from Parmenides and Plato's opponents, introduced an expression into the discussion that would better have been dealt with separately. Modern discussions of these issues take as distinct (a) the question what truth and falsity are, (b) the question what negation is, (c)questions about various uses of "is," and (d) expressions that are used to express the notions of existence and nonexistence. Dividing these questions seems the best strategy. The Equation that Plato felt obliged to accept forced him to tackle all four sorts of problems at once. In view of that, it is astonishing that he was able to do as well as he did.[34]

---

34. Scholars often write as though Plato's treatment of nonbeing was antiquity's last word on the subject. This is not true. For one thing, Aristotle plainly was not content with merely repeating Plato's solution, but tried a different attack of his own. See his *Physics* I.2–3.

# Select Bibliography

This bibiography is far from exhaustive. It includes works that have been referred to in the Introduction, as well as some more to give a rough idea of the range of works on the dialogue in the past few decades (including some that have not been referred to in the footnotes). At the end I have added a few general works on Plato and the sophists.

Ackrill, J. L. 1955, "*Symploke Eidon*," *Bulletin of the Institute of Classical Studies of the University of London*, 2:31–35.

Ackrill, J. L. 1957, "Plato and the Copula," *Journal of Hellenic Studies*, 77:1–6.

Bostock, D. 1984, "Plato on 'Is Not'," *Oxford Studies in Ancient Philosophy*, 2:89–120.

Brown, Lesley 1986, "Being in the *Sophist*," *Oxford Studies in Ancient Philosophy*, 4:49–70.

Denyer, Nicholas 1991, *Language, Thought and Falsehood in Ancient Greek Philosophy* (London: Routledge).

Detel, Wolfgang 1972, *Platons Beschreibung des falschen Satzes in Theatet und Sophistes*, *Hypomnemata*, 36 (Göttingen: Vandenhoek & Ruprecht).

Frede, Michael 1967, *Prädikation und Existenzaussage*, *Hypomnemata*, 18 (Göttingen: Vandenhoek & Ruprecht).

Gómez-Lobo, Alfonso 1975, "Platon, El Sofista: Una Seleccion Bibliografica," *Dialogos*, 28:141–51.

Gómez-Lobo, Alfonso 1977, "Plato's Description of Dialectic in the *Sophist* 253d1-e2," *Phronesis*, 22:29–47.

Gómez-Lobo, Alfonso 1979, "Platon, *Sofista* 256e5–6," *Critica*, 11:3–13.

Heinaman, Robert 1983, "Being in the *Sophist*," *Archiv für Geschichte der Philosophie*, 65:1–17.

Heinaman, Robert 1986, "Once More: Being in the *Sophist*," *Archiv für Geschichte der Philosophie*, 68:121–25.

Kahn, Charles H. 1966, "The Greek Verb 'To Be' and the Concept of Being," *Foundations of Language*, 2:245–65.

Kamlah, Wilhelm 1963, *Platons Selbstkritik im Sophistes* (Munich: Beck).

Keyt, D. 1973, "The Falsity of 'Theaetetus flies'," E. Lee, A. Mourelatos, and R. Rorty, eds., *Exegesis and Argument, Phronesis,* Supp. Vol. I, pp. 285–305.

Kostman, James 1973, "False Logos and Not-Being in Plato's *Sophist,*" J.M.E. Moravcsik, ed., *Patterns in Plato's Thought* (Dordrecht: Reidel), pp. 192–212.

Kostman, James 1989, "The Ambiguity of 'Partaking' in Plato's *Sophist,*" *Journal of the History of Philosophy,* 27:343–63.

Lee, E. N. 1972, "Plato on Negation and Not-Being in the *Sophist,*" *Philosophical Review,* 81:267–304.

Lewis, Frank 1975, "Did Plato Discover an *estin* of Identity?" *California Studies in Classical Antiquity,* 8:113–43.

Lewis, Frank 1976, "Plato on 'Not'," *California Studies in Classical Antiquity,* 9:89–115.

Lorenz, K., and Mittelstrass, J. 1966, "Theaitetos fliegt," *Archiv für Geschichte der Philosophie,* 48:113–52.

McDowell, John 1982, "Falsehood and Not-Being in Plato's *Sophist,*" Malcolm Schofield and Martha Nussbaum, eds., *Language and Logos* (Cambridge: Cambridge University Press, pp.115–34.

Malcolm, John 1967, "Plato's Analysis of *to on* and *to me on* in the *Sophist,*" *Phronesis* 12:130–46.

Malcolm, John, 1985, "Remarks on an Incomplete Rendering of Being in the *Sophist,*" *Archiv für Geschichte der Philosophie,* 67:162–65.

Meinwald, Constance 1991, *Plato's Parmenides* (New York: Oxford University Press).

Moravcsik, J.M.E. 1962, "Being and Meaning in the *Sophist,*" *Acta Philosophica Fennica,* 14:23–78.

Nehamas, Alexander 1982, "Participation and Predication in Plato's Later Thought," *Review of Metaphysics,* 36:343–74.

Owen, G.E.L. 1957, "A Proof in the *Peri Ideon,*" *Journal of Hellenic Studies,* 1957, Pt. 1:103–11, reprinted in Owen 1986.

Owen, G.E.L. 1970, "Plato on Not-Being," Vlastos 1970, pp. 223–67, reprinted in Owen 1986.

Owen, G.E.L. 1986, *Logic, Science and Dialectic,* ed. Martha Nussbaum (Ithaca: Cornell University Press).

Pelletier, Jeffrey 1990, *Parmenides, Plato, and the Semantics of Not-Being* (Chicago: University of Chicago Press).

Prauss, Gerold 1966, *Platon und der logische Eleatismus* (Berlin: de Gruyter).

Prior, William 1980, "Plato's Analysis of Being and Not-Being in the *Sophist*," *Southern Journal of Philosophy*, 18:199–211.

Reeve, C.D.C., "Motion, Rest, and Dialectic in the *Sophist*," *Archiv für Geschichte der Philosophie*, 67:47–64.

Robinson, R. 1950, "Forms and Error in Plato's *Theaetetus*," *Philosophical Review*, 59:3–30.

Rosen, Stanley 1983, *Plato's Sophist: The Drama of Original and Image* (New Haven: Yale University Press).

Russell, Bertrand 1905, "On Denoting," *Mind* 14:479–93.

Sayre, Kenneth 1976, "*Sophist* 263B Revisited," *Mind*, 85:581–86.

Sayre, Kenneth 1983, *Plato's Late Ontology* (Princeton: Princeton University Press).

Turnbull, Robert 1964, "The Argument of the *Sophist*," *Philosophical Quarterly*, 14:23–34.

Vlastos, Gregory 1965, "Degrees of Reality in Plato," Renford Bambrough, ed., *New Essays on Plato and Aristotle* (New York: Humanities Press), pp. 1–19.

Vlastos, Gregory 1970, ed., *Plato I* (Garden City: Anchor).

Vlastos, Gregory 1973, "An Ambiguity in the *Sophist*," *Platonic Studies* (Princeton: Princeton University Press), pp. 270–322.

Wallace, John 1972, "Positive, Comparative, Superlative," *The Journal of Philosophy* 69, 773–82.

White, Nicholas 1989, "Perceptual and Objective Properties in Plato," *Apeiron*, 22:45–65.

White, Nicholas 1992, "Plato's Metaphysical Epistemology," Richard Kraut, ed., *Cambridge Companion to Plato* (Cambridge: Cambridge University Press), pp. 277–310.

Wiggins, David 1970, "Sentence Meaning, Negation, and Plato's Problem of Non-Being," in Vlastos 1970, pp. 268–303.

\* \* \*

Guthrie, W.K.C. 1965–1991, *History of Greek Philosophy*, vols. I–V (Cambridge: Cambridge University Press).

Hussey, Edward 1972, *The Presocratics* (New York: Scribners).

Kerferd, G. B. 1981, *The Sophistic Movement* (Cambridge: Cambridge University Press).

Kirk, G. S., J. E. Raven, and M. Schofield, 1984, *The Presocratic Philosophers*, 3rd ed. (Cambridge: Cambridge University Press).

# Summary of the *Sophist*

216a–218b: The visitor from Elea is introduced, and the area and manner of the discussion are chosen.

218b–219a: The visitor determines that an account of the sophist is needed, but that they need to practice on an easier subject first.

219a–221c: The division leading to the definition of angling.

221c–223b: The first account of the sophist, as the hunter of rich young men.

223b–224d: The second account of the sophist, as a wholesaler of words and learning about virtue.

224d–e: The third and fourth accounts of the sophist, as the retailer seller of words and learning about virtue, made either by others or by himself.

224e–226a: The fifth account of sophistry, as the money-making branch of debating.

226a–231b: The sixth account of sophistry, as the refutation of the empty belief in one's own wisdom.

231b–e: Summary of the previous accounts of the sophist.

232a–233a: The sophist claims to engage in controversies on all subjects; but he cannot possibly know about all topics.

233a–d: So the sophist's capacity is to make people believe that they know the subjects that they engage in controversies and disputes about.

233d–234e: To make another comparison, consider a person who claims to be able to make anything, that is, someone with skill at imitation. For example, he might produce imitations by drawing, or with words.

234e–235c: Since the sophist does not know all things, he is a cheat and an imitator; so we should divide this kind up to reach an account of what he is.

235c–236d: Copy-making is divided into the making of likenesses, which are like what they are copies of, and the making of appearances, which are not.

236d–237b: But this way of describing the sophist requires speaking of what is not, which Parmenides forbade us to do.

237b–e: Can we talk about that which in no way is? An argument seems to show that anyone who tries to say that which is not is not even speaking.

238a–c: None of those which are can be applied to that which is not; but to say that which is not itself is to apply some one of those which are to it; so that which is not is completely unutterable.

238d–239c: But even when one says that that which is not is unutterable, one uses forms of words, such as singular expressions, that attribute some of that which is to it; but by the earlier argument that is impossible; so we seem to be barred from classifying the sophist as dealing with that which is not.

239c–240c: So what can it mean to say that the sophist is a copy-maker? It seems to mean that he makes a thing that is like what it is copied from, but is not really that thing, though it is a likeness of it; that seems to mean that what is not also in a way is—a kind of weaving together of that which is not with that which is.

240c–241b: Thus the sophist's ability to deceive us by appearances, as it has been formulated so far, consists precisely in his ability to engender false belief. But false belief involves believing *that which is not*, i.e., believing that *that which is not* in a way is, which the visitor takes as equivalent to believing that *that which completely is* in no way is.

241b–242a: If we are going to have any chance of giving an account of the sophist, we are going to have to take the risk of contradicting father Parmenides.

242a–243b: We need to understand what is meant by people who say that certain things are, or how many beings there are, for all such people simply advance their positions without explaining them.

243b–d: We have been assuming that, whereas we do not understand *is not*, we do understand *is*. In fact, though, we need to see what is meant by *being* too.

243d–244b: When those who say that two things are say of each of them that it is, seemingly this being must be a third thing alongside the other two things; and if so, they should tell us what it signifies.

244b–d: Likewise those who say that everything is one need to tell us what they mean by *being*. If *being* is not different from *one*, then *being* and *one* must be two names of the same thing.

244d–245b: And if *the one being* is a whole, then it must have parts, in which case it cannot be simply one.

245b–c: If it is one by having one as a characteristic, then it will not be the same as *that which is one*, and everything will be more than one. But if it is whole, not by possessing the characteristic of being whole, but by being just the whole itself, then it will not be *being*; and moreover everything will be more than one, since that which is and *the whole* will be distinct.

245c–e: On the other hand, if *the whole* is not *being* at all, then *that which is* neither is a being nor becomes a being. And there are many other problems, too, if we say that *being* is only two or one.

245e–246e: We can see the same point—that *that which is* is just as obscure as *that which is not*—by considering a dispute between two groups, the "gods," who think that only what is tangible is, and the "giants," who think that what the first group calls *being* is only *becoming*. (We may have to consider a milder version of the former group's position than they actually advocate.)

246e–247c: The gentler giants say that souls are beings, and so are the virtues of souls, such as justice and intelligence. All of these things are invisible. A soul has a kind of body, but intelligence and so forth do not.

247c–248a: Perhaps the gentle giants would accept the suggestion that a thing is just in case it has any capacity to do something or have something done to it.

248a–c: The "gods," on the other hand, think that *coming-to-be* has the capacity to do things or have things done to it, but not that being does.

248c–249b: But if a thing's being known is a case of something happening to it, they cannot say that *being* is known. In that case, however, they will have to deny that life, soul, and understanding are present in that which wholly is.

249b–c: On the other hand, there cannot be intelligence without things that stay the same and do not change.

249c–d: But since we must hold that there is intelligence and knowledge, the philosopher must reject the view of the "gods," and must say that that which is comprises both *that which rests* and *that which changes*.

249d–250c: If both *change* and *rest* are, then when we say that they are, we do not mean either that they change or that they rest, so *that which is* must be a third thing alongside them.

250c–d: This third thing, *that which is*, by its nature neither changes nor rests. But if something is not changing, it must be resting.

250d–251a: So now it is clear how confused we are about *that which is*, at least as confused as we were earlier about *that which is not*.

251a–e: We need to give an account of how we call the same thing by several names. Some young people and "late-learners" think that we cannot do this, that is, that we cannot say that a man is good, for instance, but only that good is good. Shall we then accept it that we cannot say that change or rest is? Shall we take each of these things as incapable of associating with any other, or that each associates with all, or that some associate with each other and some do not?

251e–252b: All the people who say that everything changes, and those who say that everything is an unchanging unit, and also those who say that things alternate between being unified and being divided, apply *being* to other things. None of these people could say what they want to if there were not blending.

252b–d: The same is true even of those who say that nothing can blend with anything else. Thus their position conflicts with what they say in enunciating it.

252d–e: But if we say that everything associates with everything else, then *change* will be completely at rest, and *rest* will be changing. But both of these are impossible.

252e–253c: Just as in the cases of grammar and music, it requires expertise and some kind of knowledge to tell which forms blend with each other and which do not.

253c–254b: Perhaps this is the knowledge of dialectic that the philosopher has, i.e., the knowledge of which forms are the same and which are different, of which blend with many others and which are separate from others. The sophist is hard to see because he is in the region of *that which is not*, whereas the philosopher is hard to see because his region, the region of *being*, is so bright.

254b–d: We should choose the most important forms and see which associate with which. That will help us see whether we can say that *that which is not* really is *that which is not*.

254d–e: *Change, rest,* and *that which is not* are three different kinds. The former two do not blend with each other, but the third blends with both of them.

254e–255a: And in addition to those three we have been speaking of *the same* and *the different*. All of these are distinct, and so we have a total of five kinds.

255a–b: Neither *change* nor *rest* is *the different* nor *the same*.

255b–c: *That which is* and *the same* are distinct, so *the same* is a fourth form.

255c–e: *The different* is distinct from *that which is*, and so is a fifth form.

255e–256a: *Change* is completely different from *rest*, so it is not rest.

256a: *Change* is different from *the same*, so it is not the same, but like everything else it also is the same.

256a–c: So change is the same and not the same. It is the same as itself, but because of its association with *the different*, it is separated from *the same* and so is not the same. Likewise, since *change* is different from *the same* but also different from *the different*, it is both different and not different.

256c–e: Since *change* is distinct from each of the other four kinds, it is different from *that which is*, and so it is not. But it also is, since is partakes in *that which is*. The same holds for each of the other kinds: it is not, because *the different* makes it different from *that which is*, but it also is, because it has a share in *that which is*. In this way it is possible for that which is not to be.

256e–257a: This same point applies to *that which is*: it is one thing, itself, and it is not an indefinite number of others, so it too is not. All of this comes about because it is in the nature of kinds to allow association with each other.

257a–c: When we say *not large* we do not say the contrary of the large, but something different from *the large*. Likewise, when we say *that which is not*, we do not say something contrary to *that which is*, but only something different from it. *Not* indicates something other, not something contrary.

257c–e: *The different* is divided up into parts, just as knowledge is. One part of the different is contrary to *the beautiful*; it is *the not beautiful*, and is different precisely from *the beautiful*.

257e–258b: Thus *the not beautiful* is a being contraposed to a being, and likewise in other cases. *The different* is a being, and its parts are too. A part of *the different* is a part of *being*; it is something different from *being*, but not contrary to it.

258b–e: We have done more than flout Parmenides' prohibition. Not only have we shown that those which are not are; we have also shown the form of *that which is not*, as each part of *the different* that is set over against *that which is*.

258e–259e: If anyone does not agree, he must refute our claim that different forms can blend with each other.

259e–261c: Now we need to agree about what speech is, because even if *that which is not* is, nevertheless if speech does not share in it, then the sophist will escape our account of him. If belief and speech do not associate with *that which is not*, then false speech and false belief are impossible, and if they are impossible, then so are deception and copy-making.

261d–e: Just as some things blend with each other and others do not, and likewise for letters, so too some names associate and others do not.

261e–262e: The voice can indicate things either by names or by verbs. No speech results from stringing just names together, or just verbs. But speech comes about when names and verbs are put together.

262e–263d: All speech has to be about something. "Theaetetus sits" is about Theaetetus. It is true, and thus says *that which is* about Theaetetus. "Theaetetus flies" is false, and thus says things different from *those that are* about him, and so that *those that are not* are. That is how false speech arises.

263d–264b: Thought is speech in the soul without the voice. Belief is silent affirmation or denial within the soul. When such a thing arises through perception, it is appearance, which is thus a blending of perception and belief. Since all of these are of the same kind as speech, they are capable of being false.

264b–d: The last account of the sophist recommences.

264d–265e: Now we are including sophistry under production, which can be divided into divine and human, the former producing things that come about by what is called nature, and the latter compounding things out of those things.

265e–266d: Cutting across that division, there is the division into production of originals and production of copies.

266d–268c: Copy-making is divided into likeness-making and appearance-making. Appearance-making that is done with one's own body is imitation. Imitation is informed mimicry or belief-mimicry, depending on whether it is done with knowledge or not. Belief-mimicry is either sincere or insincere. Of the latter one sort is the demagogue, and the other is the sophist.

268c: The final account of the sophist.

# Sophist

# SOPHIST

*PERSONS OF THE DIALOGUE:*
THEODORUS, SOCRATES,
VISITOR FROM ELEA, THEAETETUS

THEODORUS. We've come at the proper time by yesterday's agreement, *216* Socrates. We're also bringing this man who's visiting us. He's from Elea and he's a member of the group who gather around Parmenides and Zeno. And he's very much a philosopher.

SOCRATES. Are you bringing a visitor, Theodorus? Or are you bringing a god without realizing it instead, like the ones Homer mentions? He says gods accompany people who are respectful and just.[1] He also says the god *b* of visitors—who's at least as much a god as any other—is a companion who keeps an eye on people's actions, both the criminal and the lawful ones. So your visitor might be a greater power following along with you, a sort of god of refutation to keep watch on us and show how bad we are at speaking—and to refute us.

THD. That's not our visitor's style, Socrates. He's more moderate than the enthusiasts for debating are. And he doesn't seem to me to be a god at all. He *is* divine—but then I call all philosophers that. *c*

SOC. And that's the right thing for you to do, my friend. But probably it's no easier, I imagine, to distinguish that kind of person than it is to distinguish gods. Certainly the genuine philosophers who "haunt our cities"[2]—by contrast to the fake ones—take on all sorts of different appearances just because of other people's ignorance. As philosophers look down from above at the lives of those below them, some people think they're worthless and others think they're worth everything in the world. Sometimes they take on the appearance of statesmen, and sometimes of sophists. *d* Sometimes, too, they might give the impression that they're completely insane. But if it's all right with our visitor I'd be glad to have him tell us

Except for minor changes which are indicated in the notes, this translation follows the Oxford Classical Texts edition, edited by John Burnet. I am indebted to John M. Cooper, Gareth B. Matthews, and an anonymous reader for many helpful suggestions about the translation.

1. See Homer, *Odyssey* 9.270–71.
2. See *Odyssey* 17.483–87.

what the people where he comes from used to apply the following names
217 to, and what they thought about these things?

THD. What things?

SOC. *Sophist*, *statesman*, and *philosopher*.

THD. What, or what kind of thing, especially makes you consider asking that question? What special problem about them do you have in mind?

SOC. This: did they think that sophists, statesmen, and philosophers make up one kind of thing or two? Or did they divide them up into three kinds corresponding to the three names and attach one name to each of them?

THD. I don't think it would offend him to tell us about it. Or would it, sir?

b    THE VISITOR FROM ELEA. No, Theodorus, it wouldn't offend me. I don't have any objection. And the answer is easy: they think there are three kinds. Distinguishing clearly what each of them is, though, isn't a small or easy job.

THD. Luckily, Socrates, you've gotten hold of words that are very much like the ones we happened to be asking him about. And he made the same excuse to us that he made to you just now—since he's heard a lot about the issue, after all, and hasn't forgotten it.

c    SOC. In that case, sir, don't refuse our very first request. Tell us this. When you want to explain something to somebody, do you usually prefer to explain it by yourself in a long speech, or to do it with questions? That's the way Parmenides did it one time, when he was very old and I was young. He used questions to generate a very fine discussion.

d    VIS. It's easier to do it the second way, Socrates, if you're talking with someone who's easy to handle and isn't a trouble-maker. Otherwise it's easier to do it alone.

SOC. You can pick anyone here you want. They'll all answer you politely. But if you take my advice you'll choose one of the young ones—Theaetetus here or for that matter any of the others you prefer.

VIS. As long as I'm here with you for the first time, Socrates, I'd be
e    embarrassed not to make our meeting a conversational give-and-take, but instead to stretch things out and give a long continuous speech by myself or even to someone else, as if I were delivering an oration. A person wouldn't expect the issue you just mentioned to be as small as your question suggests. In fact it needs a very long discussion. On the other hand, it certainly seems rude and uncivilized for a visitor not to oblige you
218 and these people here, especially when you've spoken the way you have.

So I'll accept Theaetetus as the person to talk with, on the basis of your urging, and because I've talked with him myself before.

THT. Then please do that, sir, and you'll be doing us all a favor, just as Socrates said.

VIS. We probably don't need to say anything more about that, then, Theaetetus. From now on you're the one I should have the rest of our talk with. But if you're annoyed at how long the job takes, you should blame your friends here instead of me.

THT. I don't think I'll give out now, but if anything like that does *b* happen we'll have to use this other Socrates over here as a substitute. He's Socrates's namesake, but he's my age and exercises with me and he's used to sharing lots of tasks with me.

VIS. Good. As the talk goes along you'll think about that on your own. But with me I think you need to begin the investigation from the sophist— by searching for him and giving a clear account of what he is. Now in this *c* case you and I only have the name in common, and maybe we've each used it for a different thing. In every case, though, we always need to be in agreement about the thing itself by means of a verbal explanation, rather than doing without any such explanation and merely agreeing about the name. But it isn't the easiest thing in the world to grasp the tribe we're planning to search for—I mean, the sophist—or say what it is. But if an important issue needs to be worked out well, then as everyone has long thought, you need to practice on unimportant, easier issues first. So that's *d* my advice to us now, Theaetetus: since we think it's hard to hunt down and deal with the kind, *sophist*, we ought to practice our method on something easier first—unless you can tell us about another way that's somehow more promising.

THT. I can't.

VIS. Do you want us to focus on something trivial and try to use it as a pattern for the more important issue?

THT. Yes. *e*

VIS. What might we propose that's unimportant and easy to understand, but can have an account given of it just as much as more important things can? For example, *an angler*: isn't that recognisable to everybody, but not worth being too serious about?

THT. Yes.

VIS. That, I expect, will provide an appropriate method and way of *219* talking for what we want.

THT. That would be fine.

VIS. Well then, let's go after the angler from this starting point. Tell me, shall we take him to be an expert at something, or a nonexpert with another sort of capacity?

THT. He's definitely not a nonexpert.

VIS. But expertise as a whole falls pretty much into two types.

THT. How?

VIS. There's farming, or any sort of caring for any mortal body; and there's also caring for things that are put together or fabricated, which we *b* call equipment; and there's imitation. The right thing would be to call all those things by a single name.

THT. How? What name?

VIS. When you bring anything into being that wasn't in being before, we say you're a producer and that the thing you've brought into being is produced.

THT. That's right.

VIS. And all the things we went through just now have their own capacity for that.

THT. Yes.

VIS. Let's put them under the heading of production.

*c* THT. All right.

VIS. Next, consider the whole type that has to do with learning, recognition, commerce, combat, and hunting. None of these creates anything. They take things that are or have come into being, and they take possession of some of them with words and actions, and they keep other things from being taken possession of. For that reason it would be appropriate to call all the parts of this type acquisition.

THT. Yes, that would be appropriate.

*d* VIS. If every expertise falls under acquisition or production, Theaetetus, which one shall we put angling in?

THT. Acquisition, obviously.

VIS. Aren't there two types of expertise in acquisition? Is one type mutually willing exchange, through gifts and wages and purchase? And would the other type, which brings things into one's possession by actions or words, be expertise in taking possession?

THT. It seems so, anyway, given what we've said.

VIS. Well then, shouldn't we cut possession-taking in two?

THT. How?

*e* VIS. The part that's done openly we label combat, and the part that's secret we call hunting.

THT. Yes.

VIS. And furthermore it would be unreasonable not to cut hunting in two.

Tht. How?

Vis. We divide it into the hunting of living things and the hunting of lifeless things.

Tht. Yes, if there are both kinds.

Vis. How could there not be? But we should let the part involving *220* lifeless things go. It doesn't have a name, except for some kinds of diving and other trivial things like that. The other part—namely the hunting of living animals—we should call animal-hunting.

Tht. All right.

Vis. And isn't it right to say that animal-hunting has two types? One is land-hunting, the hunting of things with feet, which is divided into many types with many names. The other is aquatic hunting, which hunts animals that swim.

Tht. Of course.

Vis. And things that swim, we see, fall into things with wings and things *b* living underwater.

Tht. Of course.

Vis. And all hunting of things that have wings, I suppose, is called bird-catching.

Tht. Yes.

Vis. And all hunting of underwater things is fishing.

Tht. Yes.

Vis. Well then, this kind of hunting might be divided into two main parts.

Tht. What are they?

Vis. One of them does its hunting with stationary nets and the other one does it by striking.

Tht. What do you mean? How are you dividing them?

Vis. The first one is whatever involves surrounding something and *c* enclosing it to prevent it from escaping, so it's reasonable to call it enclosure.

Tht. Of course.

Vis. Shouldn't baskets, nets, slipknots, creels, and so forth be called enclosures?

Tht. Yes.

Vis. So we'll call this part of hunting enclosure-hunting or something like that.

Tht. Yes.

Vis. But the kind that's done by striking with hooks or three-pronged spears is different, and we should call it by one word, strike-hunting. Or *d* what term would be better?

THT. Let's not worry about the name. That one will do.

VIS. Then there's a part of striking that's done at night by firelight, and as it happens is called torch-hunting by the people who do it.

THT. Of course.

VIS. But the whole daytime part is called hooking, since even the three-pronged spears have hooks on their points.

*e*    THT. Yes, that's what it's called.

VIS. Then one part of the hooking part of striking is done by striking downward from above. And since you usually use a three-pronged spear that way, I think it's called spearing.

THT. Some people do call it that.

VIS. And I suppose there's only one type left.

THT. What?

VIS. It's the type of striking contrary to the previous one. It's done with 221 a hook, not to just any part of the fish's body but always to the prey's head and mouth, and pulls it upward from below with rods or reeds. What are we going to say its name should be, Theaetetus?

THT. I think we've now found what we said we aimed to find.

*b*    VIS. So now we're in agreement about the angler's expertise, not just as to its name; in addition we've also sufficiently grasped an account concerning the thing itself.[3] Within expertise as a whole one half was acquisitive; half of the acquisitive was taking possession; half of possession-taking was hunting; half of hunting was animal-hunting; half of animal-hunting was aquatic hunting; all of the lower portion of aquatic hunting was fishing; half of fishing was hunting by striking; and half of striking was hooking. And the part of hooking that involves a blow drawing

*c*    a thing upward from underneath is called by a name that's derived by its similarity to the action itself, that is, it's called draw-fishing or angling—which is what we're searching for.[4]

THT. We've got a completely adequate demonstration of that, anyway.

VIS. Well then, let's use that pattern to try and find the sophist, and see what he is.

THT. Fine.

VIS. The first question, then, was whether we should suppose the angler is a nonexpert, or that he's an expert at something?

---

3. Cf. 218c.

4. The Greek word is *aspalieutike*. Although the etymology of the word is in fact not known, Plato suggests, perhaps fancifully, that it comes from *ana*, "up," and *span*, "to draw."

*— What does sophistery have to do with metaphysics?*

THT. Yes.

VIS. Well, shall we suppose the sophist is a layman, or completely and    *d* truly an expert?

THT. He's not a layman at all. I understand what you're saying: he has to be the kind of person that the name *sophist* indicates.[5]

VIS. So it seems we need to take him to have a kind of expertise.

THT. But what is it?

VIS. For heaven's sake, don't we recognize that the one man belongs to the same kind as the other?

THT. Which men?

VIS. The angler and the sophist.

THT. In what way?

VIS. To me they both clearly appear to be hunters.

THT. We said which kind of hunting the angler does. What kind does    *e* the sophist do?

VIS. We divided all hunting into two parts, one for land animals and one for swimming animals.

THT. Yes.

VIS. We went through one part, about the animals that swim underwater. But we left the land part undivided, though we noted that it contains many types.

THT. Of course.    *222*

VIS. Up till that point the sophist and the angler go the same way, beginning from expertise in acquisition.

THT. They seem to, anyway.

VIS. Starting from animal hunting, though, they turn away from each other. One goes to ponds, rivers, and the sea, and hunts for the animals there.

THT. Of course.

VIS. The other one goes to the land and to different kinds of rivers, which are like plentiful meadows of wealthy youths, to take possession of the things living there.

THT. What do you mean?    *b*

VIS. There are two main kinds of things to hunt on land.

THT. What are they?

VIS. Tame things and wild ones.

THT. Is there any such thing as hunting tame animals?

---

5. The word "sophist" (*sophistes*) is etymologically related to the word "wise" (*sophos*), and so can be taken to connote knowledge and expertise.

Vis. There is if human beings are tame animals, at any rate. Make whichever assumption you like: either there are no tame animals, or there are tame animals but humans are wild, or else, you'll say, humans are tame but aren't hunted. Specify whichever you prefer to say.

*c* Tht. I think we're tame animals and I'll say that humans are in fact hunted.

Vis. Then let's say that the hunting of tame animals falls into two parts.

Tht. How?

Vis. Let's take piracy, enslavement, tyranny, along with everything that has to do with war, and let's define them all together as hunting by force.

Tht. Fine.

Vis. And we'll also take legal oratory, political oratory, and conversation *d* all together in one whole, and call them all one single sort of expertise, expertise in persuasion.

Tht. Right.

Vis. Let's say that there are two kinds of persuasion.

Tht. What are they?

Vis. One is done privately, and the other is done in public.

Tht. Yes, each of those is one type.

Vis. And doesn't one part of private hunting earn wages, while the other part gives gifts?

Tht. I don't understand.

Vis. It seems you aren't paying attention to the way lovers hunt.

Tht. In what connection?

*e* Vis. The fact that when they hunt people they give presents to them too.

Tht. Very true.

Vis. Let's call this type expertise in love.

Tht. All right.

Vis. One part of the wage-earning type approaches people by being agreeable, uses only pleasure as its bait, and earns only its own room and 223 board. I think we'd all call it flattery, or expertise in pleasing people.

Tht. Of course.

Vis. But doesn't the kind of wage-earning that actually earns money, though it claims to deal with people for the sake of virtue, deserve to be called by a different name?

Tht. Of course.

Vis. What name? Try and tell me.

Tht. It's obvious. I think we've found the sophist. I think that's the name that would be suitable for him.

Vis. So according to our account now, Theaetetus, it seems that this *b* sort of expertise belongs to appropriation, taking possession, hunting, animal-hunting, hunting on land, human hunting, hunting by persuasion, hunting privately, and money-earning.[6] It's the hunting of rich, prominent young men. And according to the way our account has turned out, it's what should be called the expertise of the sophist.

Tht. Absolutely.

Vis. Still, let's look at it this way too, since what we're looking for isn't *c* a trivial sort of expertise but quite a diverse one. And even in what we've just said earlier it actually presents the appearance of being not what we're now saying, but a different type.

Tht. How?

Vis. Expertise in acquisition had two parts, hunting and exchanging.[7]

Tht. Yes.

Vis. And let's say there are two types of exchanging, giving and selling.

Tht. All right.

Vis. And we're also going to say that selling divides in two.

Tht. How? *d*

Vis. One part is the sale of things that the seller himself makes. The other is purveying, that is, the purveying of things other people make.

Tht. Of course.

Vis. Then what? Isn't the part of purveying that's done within the city— about half of it—called retailing?

Tht. Yes.

Vis. And isn't wholesaling the part that buys and sells things for exchange between one city and another?

Tht. Of course.

Vis. And can't we see that one part of wholesaling sells things for the *e* nourishment and use of the body in exchange for cash, and the other sells things for the soul?

Tht. What do you mean by that?

Vis. Maybe we don't understand the one for the soul—since certainly we understand the other kind.

Tht. Yes.

Vis. Let's consider every kind of music that's carried from one city to *224* another and bought here and sold there, as well as painting and shows and other things for the soul. Some of them are transported and sold for

---

6. In addition to the words bracketed by Burnet, I bracket *doxopaideutikes* also.
7. Cf. 219d–e.

amusement and others for serious purposes. We can use the word *whole-saler* for the transporter and seller of these things just as well as for someone who sells food and beverages.

THT. That's absolutely true.

*b*   VIS. Wouldn't you use the same name for somebody who bought and exchanged items of knowledge for money from city to city?

THT. Definitely.

VIS. Wouldn't the right thing to say be that the art of display-oratory is one part of that soul-wholesaling? And don't we have to call another part of it, the part that consists in selling knowledge, by a name that's similar and also equally ridiculous?

THT. Definitely.

VIS. And one name should be used for the part of this knowledge-*c* selling that deals with knowledge of virtue, and another name for the part that deals with knowledge of other things?

THT. Of course.

VIS. "Expertise-selling" would fit the second one. You try and tell me the name of the first one.

THT. What other name could you mention that would fit, except for the kind, *sophist*, which we're looking for right now?[8]

VIS. I couldn't mention any other one. Come on now and let's collect it all together. We'll say that the expertise of the part of acquisition, *d* exchange, selling, wholesaling, and soul-wholesaling, dealing in words and learning that have to do with virtue—that's sophistry in its second appearance.

THT. Definitely.

VIS. In the third place I think you'd call somebody just the same thing if he settled here in the city and undertook to make his living selling those same things, both ones that he'd bought and ones that he'd made himself.

THT. Yes, I would.

*e*   VIS. So apparently you'll still say that sophistry falls under acquisition, exchange, and selling, either by retailing things that others make or by selling things that he makes himself. It's the retail sale of any learning that has to do with the sorts of things we mentioned.

THT. It has to be, since we need to stay consistent with what we said before.

---

8. Cf. above, n. 5, on the word *sophistes*.

VIS. Now let's see whether the type we're chasing is something like the following.

THT. What?

225

VIS. Combat was one part of acquisition.[9]

THT. Yes.

VIS. And it makes sense to divide it in two.

THT. How?

VIS. We'll take one part to be <u>competition</u> and the other part to be <u>fighting.</u> *What is the difference between the two?*

THT. Yes.

VIS. And it would be fitting and proper to give a name like *violence* to the part of fighting in which one body fights against another.

THT. Yes.

VIS. And as for the part that pits words against words, what else would you call it other than controversy?

THT. Nothing else.

b

*forensic (public)*
*disputation (priv)*

VIS. But we have to have two types of controversy.

THT. Why?

VIS. So far as it involves one long public speech directed against another and deals with justice and injustice, it's forensic.

THT. Yes.

VIS. But if it goes on in private discussions and is chopped up into questions and answers, don't we usually call it disputation?

THT. Yes.

VIS. One part of disputation involves controversy about contracts and isn't carried on in any systematic or expert way. We should take that to be a type of disputation, since we can express what makes it different. But it hasn't been given a name before and it doesn't deserve to get one from us.

c

THT. That's true. Its subtypes are too small and varied.

VIS. But what about disputation that's done expertly and involves controversy about general issues, including what's just and what's unjust? Don't we normally call that debating?[10]

---

9. Cf. 219e.

10. The word here translated by "debating," *eristikon* is sometimes translated (or transliterated) "eristic." It refers to a practice of competitive debating concerning various kinds of issues, often philosophical or quasi-philosophical, which the sophists made popular in Athens. Plato's use of the term stigmatizes the practice as not directed at truth (cf. Introd., Sec. 2).

THT. Of course.

*d*    VIS. Part of debating, it turns out, wastes money and the other part makes money.

THT. Absolutely.

VIS. Let's try and say what each of them ought to be called.

THT. We have to.

VIS. I think one type of debating is a result of the pleasure a person gets from the activity, and involves neglecting his own livelihood. But its style is unpleasant to most people who hear it, and in my view it's right to call it chatter. *Like bickering. No real point to it.*

THT. That's pretty much what people do call it.

*e*    VIS. You take a turn now. Say what its contrary is, which makes money from debates between individuals.

THT. How could anyone go wrong in saying that the amazing sophist we've been after has turned up once again for the fourth time.

226    VIS. It seems his type is precisely the money-making branch of expertise in debating, disputation, controversy, fighting, combat, and acquisition. According to what our account shows us now, that's the sophist.

THT. Absolutely. *So the sophist is on who can make money in his quest for the "Jems tu."*

VIS. So you see how true it is that the beast is complex and can't be caught with one hand, as they say.

THT. It does take both hands.

*b*    VIS. Yes, and you need all your capacity to follow his tracks in what's to come. Tell me: don't we call some things by names that house-servants use?

THT. A lot of things. But what are you asking about?

VIS. For example things like filtering, straining, winnowing.[11]

THT. Of course.

VIS. And also we know about carding, spinning, weaving, and a million other things like that which are involved in experts' crafts. Is that right?

*c*    THT. What general point are you trying to make with these examples?

VIS. All the things I've mentioned are kinds of dividing.

THT. Yes.

VIS. Since there's a single kind of expertise involved in all of them, then according to what I've said we'll expect it to have a single name.

THT. What shall we call it?

VIS. Discrimination.

THT. All right.

VIS. Think about whether we can see two types in it.

11. The text here is slightly garbled.

THT. You're asking me to do some quick thinking.

VIS. In fact in what we've called discriminations one kind separates        *d*
what's worse from what's better and the other separates like from like.

THT. That's obvious—now that you've said it.

VIS. I don't have an ordinary name for one of them, but I do have a
name for the kind of discrimination that leaves what's better and throws
away what's worse.

THT. What? Tell me.

VIS. I think everyone says that that kind of discrimination is cleansing.

THT. Yes.

VIS. Won't everyone see that cleansing has two types?                        *e*

THT. Yes, maybe, if they had time, but I don't see now.

VIS. Many kinds of cleansing that have to do with the body can appropri-
ately be included under a simple name.

THT. Which ones? What name?

VIS. There's the cleansing of the inside part of living bodies, which
is done by gymnastics and medicine. And there's the cleansing of the   *227*
insignificant outside part that's done by bathing. And also there's the
cleansing of nonliving bodies, which fulling and all kinds of furbishing
take care of and which have lots of specialized and ridiculous-seeming
names.

THT. Very ridiculous.

VIS. Of course, Theaetetus. But our method of dealing with words
doesn't care one way or the other whether cleansing by sponging or by
taking medicine does a lot of good or only a little. The method aims at
acquiring intelligence, so it tries to understand how all kinds of expertise   *b*
belong to the same kind or not. And so for that it values them all equally
without thinking that some of them are more ridiculous than others, as
far as their similarity is concerned. And it doesn't consider a person more
impressive because he exemplifies hunting by military expertise rather
than by picking lice. Instead it usually considers him more vapid. Moreover
you just asked about what name we call all the capacities that are assigned
to living or nonliving bodies. As far as that's concerned, it doesn't matter    *c*
to our method which name would seem to be the most appropriate, just
so long as it keeps the cleansing of the soul separate from the cleansing
of everything else. For the time being, the method has only tried to
distinguish the cleansing that concerns thinking from the other kinds—if,
that is, we understand what its aim is.

THT. I do understand, and I agree that there are two types of cleansing,
one dealing with the soul and a separate one dealing with the body.

Vis. Fine. Next listen and try to cut the one we've mentioned in two.

*d*    Tht. I'll try to follow your lead and cut it however you say.

Vis. Do we say that wickedness in the soul is something different from virtue?

Tht. Of course.

Vis. And to cleanse something was to leave what's good and throw out whatever's inferior.

Tht. Yes.

Vis. So insofar as we can find some way to remove what's bad in the soul, it will be suitable to call it cleansing.

Tht. Of course.

Vis. We have to say that there are two kinds of badness that affect the soul.

Tht. What are they?

228   Vis. One is like bodily sickness, and the other is like ugliness.

Tht. I don't understand.

Vis. Presumably you regard sickness and discord as the same thing, don't you?

Tht. I don't know what I should say to that.

Vis. Do you think that discord is just dissension among things that are naturally of the same kind, and arises out of some kind of corruption?

Tht. Yes.

Vis. And ugliness is precisely a consistently unattractive sort of dispro- portion?

*b*    Tht. Yes.

Vis. Well then, don't we see that there's dissension in the souls of people in poor condition, between beliefs and desires, anger and pleasures, reason and pains, and all of those things with each other?

Tht. Absolutely.

Vis. But all of them do have to be akin to each other.

Tht. Of course.

Vis. So we'd be right if we said that wickedness is discord and sickness of the soul.

Tht. Absolutely right.

*c*    Vis. Well then, suppose something that's in motion aims at a target and tries to hit it, but on every try passes by it and misses. Are we going to say that it does this because it's properly proportioned or because it's out of proportion?

Tht. Out of proportion, obviously.

Vis. But we know that no soul is willingly ignorant of anything.

THT. Definitely.

VIS. But ignorance occurs precisely when a soul tries for the truth, but   *d*
swerves aside from understanding and so is beside itself.[12]

THT. Of course.

VIS. So we have to take it that an ignorant soul is ugly and out of
proportion.

THT. It seems so.

VIS. Then there are, it appears, these two kinds of badness in the soul.
Most people call one of them wickedness, but it's obviously a disease of
the soul.

THT. Yes.

VIS. They call the other one ignorance, but if it occurs only in a person's
soul they aren't willing to agree that it's a form of badness.

THT. One thing absolutely must be granted—the point I was in doubt   *e*
about when you made it just now—that there are two kinds of deficiency
in the soul. We need to say that cowardice, licentiousness, and injustice
are a disease in us, and that to be extremely ignorant of all sorts of things
is a kind of ugliness.

VIS. In the case of the body, weren't there two kinds of expertise dealing
with those two conditions?

THT. What were they?

VIS. Gymnastics for ugliness and medicine for sickness.   *229*

THT. Apparently.

VIS. And isn't correction the most appropriate of all kinds of expertise
for treating insolence, injustice, and cowardice?[13]

THT. So it seems, to judge by what people think.

VIS. Well then, for all kinds of ignorance wouldn't teaching be the right
treatment to mention?

THT. Yes.

VIS. Now should we say that there's only one kind of expertise in   *b*
teaching or more than one, with two of them being the most important
ones? Think about it.

THT. I am.

VIS. I think we'll find it quickest this way.

---

12. The point here is to claim a connection between internal disproportion and external
failure. Cf. Campbell's note on the passage. *Paraphrosyne* is a quite strong word, which means
"being beside oneself" or "derangement."

13. It seems to me that the text is faulty here. Neither Cobet's *Dikei* nor the mss reading
*dike* is satisfactory. The general sense, however, is clear.

THT. How?

VIS. By seeing whether ignorance has a cut down the middle of it. If it has two parts, that will force teaching to have two parts too, one for each of the parts of ignorance.

THT. Well, do you see what we're looking for?

c    VIS. I think I see a large, difficult type of ignorance marked off from the others and overshadowing all of them.

THT. What's it like?

VIS. Not knowing, but thinking that you know. That's what probably causes all the mistakes we make when we think.

THT. That's true.

VIS. And furthermore it's the only kind of ignorance that's called lack of learning.

THT. Certainly.

VIS. Well then, what should we call the part of teaching that gets rid of it?

d    THT. The other part consists in the teaching of crafts, I think, and there we call it education.

VIS. And just about all other Greeks do too, Theaetetus. But we still have to think about whether education is indivisible or has divisions that are worth mentioning.

THT. We do have to think about that.

VIS. I think it can be cut somehow.

THT. How?

e    VIS. One part of the kind of teaching that's done in words is a rough road, and the other part is smoother.

THT. What do you mean by these two parts?

VIS. One of them is our forefathers' time-honored method of scolding or gently encouraging. They used to employ it especially on their sons, 230 and many still use it on them nowadays when they do something wrong. Admonition would be the right thing to call all of this.

THT. Yes.

VIS. As for as the other part, some people seem to have an argument to give to themselves that lack of learning is always involuntary, and that if someone thinks he's wise, he'll never be willing to learn anything about what he thinks he's clever at. These people think that though admonition is a lot of work, it doesn't do much good.

THT. They're right about that.

b    VIS. So they set out to get rid of the belief in one's own wisdom in another way.

THT. How?

VIS. They cross-examine someone when he thinks he's saying something though he's saying nothing. Then, since his opinions will vary inconsistently, these people will easily scrutinize them. They collect his opinions together during the discussion, put them side by side, and show that they conflict with each other at the same time on the same subjects in relation to the same things and in the same respects. The people who are being examined see this, get angry at themselves, and become calmer toward others. They lose their inflated and rigid beliefs about themselves *c* that way, and no loss is pleasanter to hear or has a more lasting effect on them. Doctors who work on the body think it can't benefit from any food that's offered to it until what's interfering with it from inside is removed. The people who cleanse the soul, my young friend, likewise think the soul, too, won't get any advantage from any learning that's offered to it until *d* someone shames it by refuting it, removes the opinions that interfere with learning, and exhibits it cleansed, believing that it knows only those things that it does know, and nothing more.

THT. That's the best and most healthy-minded way to be.

VIS. For all these reasons, Theaetetus, we have to say that refutation is the principal and most important kind of cleansing. Conversely we have to think that even the king of Persia, if he remains unrefuted, is uncleansed *e* in the most important respect. He's also uneducated and ugly, in just the ways that anyone who is going to be really happy has to be completely clean and beautiful.

THT. Absolutely.

VIS. Well then, who are we going to say the people who apply this form of expertise are? I'm afraid to call them sophists. *231*

THT. Why?

VIS. So we don't pay sophists too high an honor.

THT. But there's a similarity between a sophist and what we've been talking about.

VIS. And between a wolf and a dog, the wildest thing there is and the gentlest. If you're going to be safe, you have to be especially careful about similarities, since the type we're talking about is very slippery. Still, let that stand. When the sophists are enough on their guard I don't think they'll dispute about an unimportant distinction. *b*

THT. That seems right.

VIS. So let it be the cleansing part of the expertise of discriminating things; and let it be marked off as the part of that which concerns souls; and within that it's teaching; and within teaching it's education. And let's say that within education, according to the way the discussion has turned now, the refutation of the empty belief in one's own wisdom is nothing other than our noble sophistry.[14]

THT. Let's say that. But the sophist has appeared in lots of different
c ways. So I'm confused about what expression or assertion could convey the truth about what he really is.

VIS. You're right to be confused. But we have to think that he's extremely confused, too, about where he can go to escape from our account of him. The saying that you can't escape all your pursuers is right. So now we really have to go after him.

THT. Right.

VIS. But let's stop first and catch our breath, so to speak. And while
d we're resting let's ask ourselves, "Now, how many different appearances has the sophist presented to us?" I think we first discovered him as a hired hunter of rich young men.[15]

THT. Yes.

VIS. Second, as a wholesaler of learning about the soul.[16]

THT. Right.

VIS. Third, didn't he appear as a retailer of the same things?[17]

THT. Yes, and fourth as a seller of his own learning?[18]

VIS. Your memory's correct. I'll try to recall the fifth way: he was an
e athlete in verbal combat, distinguished by his expertise in debating.[19]

THT. Yes.

VIS. The sixth appearance was disputed, but still we made a concession to him and took it that he cleanses the soul of beliefs that interfere with learning.[20]

THT. Definitely.

232 VIS. Well then, suppose people apply the name of a single sort of expertise to someone, but he appears to have expert knowledge of lots of things. In a case like that don't you notice that something's wrong with the the way he appears? Isn't it obvious that if somebody takes him to be an expert at many things, then that observer can't be seeing clearly what

14. The text here seems defective, but the general sense is clear.

15. See 221c–223b.

16. See 223c–224d.

17. See 224d–e.

18. See 224d–e.

19. See 224e–226a.

20. See 226a–231b.

it is in his expertise that all of those many pieces of learning focus on—which is why he calls him by many names instead of one?

THT. That definitely does seem to be the nature of the case.

VIS. So let's not let laziness make that happen to us. First let's take up *b* one of the things we said about the sophist before, which seemed to me to exhibit him especially clearly.

THT. What is it?

VIS. We said that he engages in controversies, didn't we?

THT. Yes.

VIS. And also that he teaches other people to do the same thing too?

THT. Of course.

VIS. Then let's think: what subject do people like him claim to make others able to engage in controversies about? Let's start with something like this: do sophists make people competent to engage in controversies *c* on issues about the gods, which are opaque to most people?

THT. Well, people say they do.

VIS. And also things that are obvious, on the earth and in the sky, and related matters?

THT. Of course.

VIS. And when people make general statements in private discussions about being and coming-to-be, we know that sophists are clever at engaging in controversies with them and they also make other people able to do the same thing?

THT. Absolutely.

VIS. And what about laws and all kinds of political issues? Don't sophists *d* promise to make people capable of engaging in disputes about them?

THT. If they didn't promise that, practically no one would bother to discuss anything with them.

VIS. As a matter of fact you can find anything you need to say to provoke a controversy with any expert himself, both in general and within each particular field, laid out published and written down for anybody who wants to learn it.

THT. Apparently you're talking about Protagoras' writings on wrestling and other fields of expertise. *e*

VIS. And on many other things, too, my friend. In fact, take expertise in controversy as a whole. Doesn't it seem like a capacity that's sufficient for carrying on disputes about absolutely everything?

THT. It doesn't seem to leave much of anything out, anyway.

VIS. But for heaven's sake, my boy, do you think that's possible? Or maybe you young people see into this issue more keenly than we do.

*233*   THT.  Into what? What are you getting at? I don't fully understand what you're asking.

VIS.  Whether it's possible for any human being to know everything.

THT.  If it were, sir, we'd be very well off.

VIS.  But how could someone who didn't know about a subject make a sound objection against someone who knew about it?

THT.  He couldn't.

VIS.  Then what is it in the sophist's capacity that's so amazing?

THT.  About what?

*b*   VIS.  How the sophists can ever make young people believe they're wiser than everyone else about everything. It's obvious that they didn't make correct objections against anyone, or didn't appear so to young people. Or if they did appear to make correct objections, but their disputing didn't make them look any the wiser for it, then—just as you say—people would hardly be willing to pay them money to become their students.

THT.  Right.

VIS.  But people are willing to?

THT.  They certainly are.

*c*   VIS.  Since sophists do seem, I think, to know about the things they engage in controversies about.

THT.  Of course.

VIS.  And they do it, we say, about every subject?

THT.  Yes.

VIS.  So to their students they appear wise about everything?

THT.  Of course.

VIS.  But without actually being wise—since that appeared impossible.

THT.  Of course it's impossible.

VIS.  So the sophist has now appeared as having a kind of belief-knowledge[21] about everything, but not truth.

*d*   THT.  Absolutely. What you've said about them is probably just right.

VIS.  But let's consider a pattern that will exhibit them more clearly.

THT.  What pattern is that?

VIS.  This one. Pay attention to me, and try to do a good job of answering my questions.

THT.  Which questions?

VIS.  If someone claimed that by a single kind of expertise he could

---

21. Plato's phrase is *doxastike episteme*. *Doxa* is his normal word for "belief" or "opinion," and "*episteme*" is his normal word for "knowledge" or "understanding." Cf. *Rep.* 475–80.

know, not just how to say things or to engage in controversies with people, but how to make and do everything, then . . .

THT. What do you mean, *everything?*[22]                                        e

VIS. You don't understand the first thing I say! Seemingly you don't understand *everything!*

THT. No, I don't.

VIS. Well, I mean *everything* to include you and me and also the other animals and plants . . .

THT. What are you talking about?

VIS. If someone claimed that he'd make you and me and all the other living things . . .

THT. What kind of making are you talking about? You're not talking   234 about some kind of gardener—after all, you did say he made animals.

VIS. Yes, and also I mean the sea and earth and heaven and gods and everything else. And furthermore he makes them each quickly and sells them at a low price.

THT. You're talking about some kind of game for schoolchildren.

VIS. Well, if someone says he knows everything and would teach it to someone else cheaply and quickly, shouldn't we think it's a game?

THT. Of course.

VIS. Do you know of any game that involves more expertise than imita-   b
tion does, and is more engaging?

THT. No, not at all, since you've collected everything together and designated a very broad, extremely diverse type.

VIS. So think about the man who promises he can make everything by means of a single kind of expertise. Suppose that by being expert at drawing he produces things that have the same names as real things. Then we know that when he shows his drawings from far away he'll be able to fool the more mindless young children into thinking that he can actually produce anything he wants to.

---

22. Emphasis is used in this translation for several different things, which are not distinguished in the Greek. Sometimes it represents quotation, indicating that Plato is talking about a word or other linguistic expression. At other times it indicates that he is talking about a concept that a linguistic expression expresses, or else about a property or attribute that it signifies. In some cases of this sort he is talking about a Form, in the sense of his doctrine in the *Phaedo* and the *Republic* (see below, n. 26). Greek did not have the orthographic device of quotation marks (and except for one clumsy and seldom-used device, no good brief way of indicating quotation explicitly at all). Moreover Plato never developed a standard device that he consistently used to designate a concept, or a property, or a Form. As a result, the reader must do some tricky interpreting to decide what he *is* talking about.

*c*   THT. Of course.

VIS. Well then, won't we expect that there's another kind of expertise—this time having to do with words—and that someone can use it to trick young people when they stand even farther away from the truth about things? Wouldn't he do it by putting words in their ears, and by showing them spoken images of everything, so as to make them believe that the words are true and that the person who's speaking to them is the wisest person there is?

*d*   THT. Yes, why shouldn't there be that kind of expertise too?

VIS. So, Theaetetus, suppose enough time has passed and the sophist's hearers have gotten older, and that they approach closer to real things and are forced by their experiences to touch up palpably against them.[23] Won't most of them inevitably change their earlier beliefs, which made large things appear small and easy things appear hard?[24] And won't the facts
*e*   they've encountered in the course of their actions completely overturn all the appearances that had come to them in the form of words?

THT. Yes—at least as far as what someone my age can tell. But I think I'm one of the young people who are still standing far away from real things.

VIS. That's why all of us here will keep trying to take you as close to them as possible, but without your needing those experiences to force you.
235  But tell me about the sophist. Is it obvious by now that he's a kind of cheat who imitates real things? Or are we still in any doubt about whether he truly knows all the things that he seems to be able to engage in controversies about?

THT. But, sir, how could we be in any doubt? By this time it's pretty obvious from what we've said that he's one of those people who play games.

VIS. So we have to regard him as a cheat and an imitator.

THT. How could we avoid it?

VIS. Well, now it's our job not to let the beast escape. We've almost
*b*   hemmed him in with one of those net-like devices that words provide for things like this. So anyway he won't get away from this next point.

THT. What is it?

23. In 259d Plato alludes to this passage.

24. The text in d6–7 cannot mean what, e.g., Diès and Cornford take it to mean, that "what seemed important will not appear trifling. . . ." For example *megala* by itself, even in this context, cannot mean "what *seemed* important" (cf., e.g., *Phdo.* 74b7–8). If the present text is right, one must read no comma after *doxas* and take the *hoste* clause with *genomenas.*

VIS. From being taken to be a kind of magician.

THT. That's what he seems to me to be too.

VIS. So it's settled. We'll divide the craft of copy-making as quickly as we can and we'll go down into it. Then if the sophist gives up right away we'll obey the royal commandand we'll capture him and hand our catch     *c* over to the king. But if the sophist slips down somewhere into the parts of the craft of imitation, we'll follow along with him and we'll divide each of the parts that contain him until we catch him.[25] Anyway, neither he nor any other kind will ever be able to boast that he's escaped from the method of people who are able to chase a thing through both the particular and the general.

THT. Good. That's how we have to do it.

VIS. Going by the method of division that we've used so far, Ithink I see two types of imitation here too. But I don't think I can clearly tell yet     *d* which one the type or form[26] we're looking for is in.

THT. Well, first tell us what distinction you mean.

VIS. One type of imitation I see is the art of likeness-making. That's the one we have whenever someone produces an imitation by keeping to the proportions of length, breadth, and depth of his model, and also by     *e* keeping to the appropriate colors of its parts.

THT. But don't all imitators try to do that?

VIS. Not the ones who sculpt or draw very large works. If they reproduced the true proportions of their beautiful subjects, you see, the upper parts would appear smaller than they should, and the lower parts would     *236* appear larger, because we see the upper parts from farther away and the lower parts from closer.

THT. Of course.

VIS. So don't those craftsmen say goodbye to truth, and produce in their images the proportions that seem to be beautiful instead of the real ones?

THT. Absolutely.

---

25. For a discussion of the allusion see Dies's note.

26. In its first occurrence here "type" translates *eidos*, and then "type or form" translates *idea*. In the rest of this translation both "type" and "form" are used for both of these words. Both words are often used in connection with Plato's doctrine of "Forms" as it is enunciated in the *Phaedo* and the *Republic*. In 248a Plato is obviously alluding to the sense of *eidos* involved in that doctrine. It cannot be assumed without argument, however, that the same is true of all occurrences of the two words in the *Sophist*. For problems surrounding the words see Introduction, pp. xii–xiv.

Vis. So can't the first sort of image be called a likeness, since it's like the thing?

Tht. Yes.

*b* Vis. And as we said before, the part of imitation that deals with that should be called likeness-making.

Tht. Yes.

Vis. Now, what are we going to call something that appears to be like a beautiful thing, but only because it's seen from a viewpoint that's not beautiful, and would seem unlike the thing it claims to be like if you came to be able to see such large things adequately? If it appears the way the thing does but in fact isn't like it, isn't it an appearance?

Tht. Of course.

*c* Vis. And this part of imitation covers a great deal of painting and of the rest of imitation.

Tht. Of course.

Vis. Wouldn't *appearance-making* be the right thing to call expertise in producing appearances that aren't likenesses?

Tht. Yes, definitely.

Vis. Well, these are the two types of copy-making I meant, likeness-making and appearance-making.

Tht. You were right about that.

Vis. But still I can't see clearly the thing I was in doubt about then,[27] namely, which type we should put the sophist in. He's really an amazing man—very hard to make out. He's still escaped neatly into an impossibly confusing type to search through.

*d*

Tht. It seems that way.

Vis. Are you agreeing with me because you know that, or is the current dragging you, so to speak, into agreement so quickly because the discussion has given you a habit of agreeing?

Tht. What do you mean? Why do you say that?

Vis. Really, my young friend, this is a very difficult investigation we're engaged in. This appearing, and this seeming but not being, and this saying things but not true things—all these issues are full of confusion, just as they always have been. It's extremely hard, Theaetetus, to say what form of speech we should use to say that there really is such a thing as false saying or believing, and moreover to utter this without being caught in a verbal conflict.

*e*

*237*

Tht. Why?

27. See 235d.

Vis. Because this form of speech of ours involves the rash assumption that *that which is not* is, since otherwise falsity wouldn't come into being. But when we were boys, my boy, the great Parmenides testified to us from start to finish, speaking in both prose and poetic rhythyms that

Never shall this force itself on us, that that which is not may be;
While you search, keep your thought far away from this path.[28]

So we have his testimony to this. And our own way of speaking[29] itself would make the point especially obvious if we examined it a little. So if it's all the same to you, let's look at that first.                                                                 *b*

Tht. As far as I'm concerned you can do what you want. But as far as our way of speaking is concerned, think about how it will go best, and follow along with it and take me along the road with you.

Vis. That's what we have to do. Tell me: do we dare to utter the sound *that which in no way is?*

Tht. Of course.

Vis. But suppose one of our listeners weren't debating or playing a game but had to think seriously and answer the following question: What should the name, *that which is not*, be applied to? Why do we think he'd     *c*
use it, and in what connection, and for what kind of purpose? And what would he indicate by it to someone else who wanted to find out about it?

---

28. See Parmenides, frag. 7, ll.1–2. The same lines reoccur, with one slight textual differ-ence, at 258d. The text there is probably the more correct representation of what Parmenides wrote, but it seems most likely that Plato quoted the lines in two different ways.

29. "Way of speaking" here translates *logos*—a notoriously problematical Greek word, which elsewhere in the translation appears also as "words," "speech," and "account," and can sometimes mean "(linguistic or verbal) expression," "definition," "sentence," "statement," and the like. It is cognate with the verb *legein*, "to say," and is frequently used in connection with it here, so that the connection between *logos* and speaking is never lost from clear view. Because Plato is concerned mainly with the possibility of saying things that are false, the items referred to by *logos* are often (false) statements or sentences. *Logos* itself, however, is broader than either of these two words in English. Cf. n. 74.

As Plato makes clear, the problem about *that which is not* that he is formulating here emerges in the fact that attempts to produce a linguistic expression that unproblematically conveys the notion of *that which is not* seem to involve something like a contradiction (cf. Introd., pp. xx–xxi). (This is not to say, however, that he thinks that the problem is wholly generated by language or is fundamentally linguistic. As I understand him, he takes it to be a metaphysical problem about how things are, which is reflected in, but not created by, certain linguistic phenomena.)

THT. That's a hard question. In fact, it's just about completely, impossibly confusing for someone like me to answer.

VIS. But anyway this much is obvious to us, that *that which is not* can't be applied to any of *those which are*.[30]

THT. Of course not.

VIS. So if you can't apply it to *that which is*, it wouldn't be right either to apply it to *something*.

THT. Why not?

d  VIS. It's obvious to us that we always apply this *something* to a *being*, since it's impossible to say it by itself, as if it were naked and isolated from all *beings*.[31] Isn't that right?

THT. Yes.

VIS. Are you agreeing because you're thinking that a person who says *something* has to be saying some *one* thing?

THT. Yes.

VIS. Since you'd say that *something* is a sign of *one*, and that *a couple of things* is a sign of *two*, and *somethings* is a sign of *plurality*?

THT. Of course.

e  VIS. And it's absolutely necessary, it seems, that someone who does not say *something* says *nothing*[32] at all.

THT. Yes.

VIS. Therefore don't we have to refuse to admit that a person like that speaks but says *nothing*? Instead, don't we have to deny that anyone who tries to utter *that which is not* is even speaking?

THT. Then our way of speaking would have reached the height of confusion.

238  VIS. Don't do any boasting yet. There are still more confusions to come, including the primary and most fundamental one, which actually happens to be at the source of the whole problem.

THT. What do you mean? Don't hold back. Tell me.

VIS. To *that which is* there might belong some other of *those which are*.

THT. Of course.

VIS. But shall we say that any of *those which are* can ever belong to *that which is not*?

THT. How could they?

---

30. The text here is the result of an emendation, though a reasonably secure one.

31. The text here is somewhat problematical.

32. Note that the Greek word for "nothing," *meden*, literally means something like "not even one" (*mede hen*).

Vis. Now then, we take all the numbers to be *beings*.

Tht. Yes, if we take anything else to be.                              *b*

Vis. Then let's not even try to apply either *plurality* of number or *one* to *that which is not*.

Tht. Our way of speaking itself tells us that it would be wrong to try to.

Vis. Then how would anyone try either to say *those which are not* or *that which is not* out loud, or even grasp them in thought, apart from number?

Tht. Tell me.

Vis. Whenever we speak of *those which are not*, aren't we trying to apply   *c* numerical *plurality* to them?

Tht. Of course.

Vis. And when we speak of *that which is not* aren't we applying *one* to it?

Tht. Obviously.

Vis. But we say it isn't either right or correct to try to attach *that which is* to *that which is not*.

Tht. That's absolutely true.

Vis. Do you understand, then, that it's impossible to say, speak, or think *that which is not* itself correctly by itself? It's unthinkable, unsayable, unutterable, and unformulable in speech.

Tht. Absolutely.

Vis. So was I wrong just now when I said that I would formulate the   *d* biggest confusion about it, when we have this other one to state which is even bigger?

Tht. What is it?

Vis. My good young friend, don't you notice on the basis of the things we said that *that which is not* even confuses the person who's refuting it in just this way, that whenever someone tries to refute it, he's forced to say mutually contrary things about it?

Tht. What do you mean? Say it more clearly.

Vis. You shouldn't expect more clarity from me. I was the one who made the statement that *that which is not* should not share either in *one* or   *e* in *plurality*. But even so I've continued after all that to speak of it as *one*, since I say *that which is not*. You understand?

Tht. Yes.

Vis. And again a little earlier I said that it *is* unutterable, unsayable, and inexpressible in speech. Do you follow?

Tht. I follow, of course.

Vis. So in trying to attach *being* to it wasn't I saying things that were   *239* the contrary of what I'd said before?

THT. Apparently.

VIS. And in attaching *that which*,[33] wasn't I speaking of it as *one*?

THT. Yes.

VIS. And also in speaking of it as something inexpressible in speech, unsayable, and unutterable, I was speaking of it as one thing.

THT. Of course.

VIS. But we say that if someone speaks correctly he shouldn't definitely fix it as either one or plural. He shouldn't even call it *it* at all, since even calling it by that label he'd be addressing it by means of the form, *one*.

THT. Absolutely.

*b*  VIS. Then what would somebody say about me? He'd find that the refutation of *that which is not* has been defeating me for a long time. So, as I said, let's not use what I say to help us think of how to speak correctly about *that which is not*. Come on, let's use what you say instead.

THT. What do you mean?

VIS. Come on, pull yourself together for us as well as you can and try it—since you're young. Try to say something correct about *that which is not*, without attaching either *being*, *one*, or numerical *plurality* to it.

*c*  THT. I'd have to have a strangely large amount of enthusiasm for the project to try it myself after seeing what you've gone through.

VIS. Well, let's give up on both you and me, if you prefer. But until we meet someone who can do it let's say that the sophist has stopped at nothing. He's escaped down into inaccessible confusion.

THT. He certainly seems to have.

VIS. So if we say he has some expertise in appearance-making, it will

*d*  be easy for him to grab hold of our use of words in return and twist our words in the contrary direction. Whenever we call him a copy-maker he'll ask us what in the world we mean by a "copy." We need to think, Theaetetus, about how to answer the young man's question.

THT. Obviously we'll say we mean copies in water and mirrors, and also copies that are drawn and stamped and everything else like that.

*e*  VIS. Evidently, Theaetetus, you haven't seen a sophist.

THT. Why do you say that?

VIS. He'll seem to you to have his eyes shut, or else not to have any eyes at all.

THT. How?

---

33. I accept Cornford's conjecture *to* "*to.*" I translate it by "that which" because I take it as part of the phrase *to me on*, which I generally translate by "that which is not." In Greek the form is singular (in contrast with *ta*, for example, "those which").

VIS. He'll laugh at what you say when you answer him that way, with talk about things in mirrors or sculptures, and when you speak to him as if he could see. He'll pretend he doesn't know about mirrors or water or *240* even sight, and he'll put his question to you only in terms of words.

THT. What sort of question?

VIS. He'll ask about what runs through all those things which you call many, but which you thought you should call by the one name, *copy*, to cover them all, as if they were all one thing. Say something, then, and defend yourself, and don't give any ground to him.

THT. What in the world would we say a copy is, sir, except something that's made similar to a true thing and is another thing that's like it? *b*

VIS. You're saying it's another *true* thing like it? Or what do you mean by *like it*?

THT. Not that it's *true* at all, but that it resembles the true thing.

VIS. Meaning by *true*, *really being*?

THT. Yes.

VIS. And meaning by *not true*, *contrary of true*?

THT. Of course.

VIS. So you're saying that *that which is like* is not really *that which is*, if you speak of it as *not true*.

THT. But it *is*, in a way.

VIS. But not truly, you say.

THT. No, except that it really is a likeness.

VIS. So it's not really *what is*, but it really is what we call a likeness?

THT. Maybe *that which is not* is woven together with *that which is* in *c* some way like that—it's quite bizarre.

VIS. Of course it's strange. Anyway, you can see that the many-headed sophist is still using this interweaving to force us to agree unwillingly that *that which is not* in a way is.[34]

THT. I definitely do see it.

VIS. Well then, how can we define his field of expertise, so as to be consistent?

THT. What do you mean? What kind of problem are you afraid of?

VIS. When we say that he deceives us about appearances and that he's *d* an expert at deception, are we saying so because his expertise makes our souls believe what is false? Or what shall we say?

THT. Just that. What else would we say?

---

34. In 241d, the Visitor will himself say that this is what we have to say. See also Introduction.

Vis. Again, a false belief will be a matter of believing things that are contrary to *those which are*? Or what?

Tht. Yes, contrary.

Vis. So you're saying that a false belief is believing *those which are not*.

Tht. Necessarily.

*e*   Vis. Believing that *those which are not* are not, or that *those which in no way are* in a way are?

Tht. That *those which are not* are in a way, it has to be, if anyone is ever going to be even a little bit wrong.

Vis. Well, doesn't a false belief also believe that *those which completely are* in no way are?[35]

Tht. Yes.

Vis. And this is false too?

Tht. Yes.

*241*   Vis. And I think we'll also regard false speaking the same way, as saying that *those which are* are not, and that *those which are not* are.

Tht. How else would it be false?

Vis. I don't suppose there's any other way. The sophist, though, is going to deny that this way is possible. And how could any sensible person accept it, now that what we agreed to earlier has been reinforced.[36] Do we understand what he's saying, Theaetetus?

Tht. How could we not understand that when dare to say that falsity is in beliefs and words contain falsity, we're saying what is contrary to
*b*   what we said just before. We're forced to attach *that which is* to *that which is not*, even though we agreed just now[37] that that's completely impossible.

Vis. Your memory's correct. But think about what we need to do about the sophist. You see how many and easily available his supply of objections and confusions is if we assume, as we search for him, that he's an expert at cheating and falsehood-making.

Tht. Definitely.

*c*   Vis. He's got a practically infinite supply of them, and we've gone through only a small fraction.

Tht. If so, then it seems it would be impossible to catch him.

Vis. What, then? Are we going to go soft and give up?

---

35. Notice that the Visitor's formulation goes beyond what Theaetetus has just maintained, and says that believing falsely requires believing that *those which* **completely** *are* in *no* way are. See Introd., Sec. 7.

36. I.e., 237a–238c, reinforced by 238d–239c.

37. In 238a.

THT. I say we shouldn't, if there's even the smallest chance that we can catch him.

VIS. So you'll be forgiving and, as you said, happy if we can somehow extricate ourselves even slightly from such a powerful argument?

THT. Of course.

VIS. Then I've got something even more urgent to request.  *d*

THT. What?

VIS. Not to think that I'm turning into some kind of patricide.

THT. What do you mean?

VIS. In order to defend ourselves we're going to have to subject father Parmenides' saying to further examination, and insist by brute force both that *that which is not* somehow is, and then again that *that which is* somehow is not.[38]

THT. It does seem that when we say what we're going to say, we'll to have to fight through that issue.

VIS. That's obvious even to a blind man, as they say. We'll never be  *e* able to avoid having to make ourselves ridiculous by saying conflicting things whenever we talk about false statements and beliefs, either as copies or likenesses or imitations or appearances, or about whatever sorts of expertise there are concerning those things—unless, that is, we either refute Parmenides' claims or else agree to accept them.

THT. That's true.

VIS. So that's why we have to be bold enough to attack what our father  *242* says. Or, if fear keeps us from doing that, then we'll have to leave it alone completely.

THT. Fear, anyway, isn't going to stop us.

VIS. Well then, I've got a third thing to ask you, something small.

THT. Just tell me what it is.

VIS. When I was talking a minute ago I said that I've always given up whenever I've tried to refute what Parmenides said, just the way I did this time.

THT. Yes, you did say that.

VIS. I'm afraid I'll seem insane to you if I'm always shifting my position back and forth, given what I've said. It's for your sake that we'll be trying  *b* to refute what Parmenides said—*if* we can do it.

THT. Go ahead, then. Don't worry about that. I won't think you're behaving inappropriately in any way if you go right ahead with your refutation and demonstration.

38. Cf. 240c.

VIS. Well then, how shall I begin this dangerous discussion? The path we absolutely have to turn onto, my boy, is this.[39]

THT. Namely, . . . ?

VIS. We have to reexamine things that have seemed completely clear
*c* to us till now. That way we won't be confused about them, and our mistaken belief that we understand them well won't make us reach agreement too quickly.

THT. Say what you mean more clearly.

VIS. Parmenides' way of talking to us has been rather easygoing, it seems to me. So does the way of talking that everyone uses who has ever urged us to specify just how many beings there are and what they're like.

THT. How?

VIS. They each appear to me to tell us a myth, as if we were children. One tells us that there are three beings, and that sometimes they're
*d* somehow at war with each other, while at other times they become friendly, marry, give birth, and bring up their offspring.[40] Another one says that there are two beings, wet and dry or hot and cold. He marries them off and makes them set up house together.[41] And our Eleatic tribe, starting from Xenophanes and even people before him, tells us their myth on the assumption that what they call "all things" are just one.[42] Later on, some
*e* Ionian and Sicilian muses both had the idea that it was safer to weave the two views together. They say that *that which is* is both many and one, and is bound by both hatred and friendship. According to the terser of these muses, in being taken apart they're brought together.[43] The more relaxed muses, though, allow things to be free from that condition sometimes. They say that all that there is alternates, and that sometimes it's one and
243 friendly under Aphrodite's influence,[44] but at other times it's many and at war with itself because of some kind of strife.[45] It's hard to say whether any one of these thinkers has told us the truth or not, and it wouldn't be

39. Plato here alludes to Parmenides' wording in the lines quoted at 237a and 258d.

40. It cannot be determined whom Plato has in mind here.

41. Nor can it be said for certain who is meant here; one possibility is Ion (see Isocrates XV.268).

42. This group includes Parmenides of Elea (the Visitor, of course, comes from there).

43. The reference here is to Heraclitus, who was Ionian. See frag. 51 (cf. Plato, *Symp.* 187a).

44. Aphrodite was the goddess of love.

45. Here Plato refers to Empedocles, who lived in Sicily.

appropriate for us to be critical of such renowned and venerable men. But it wouldn't be offensive to note the following thing, either.

THT. What?

VIS. That they've been inconsiderate and contemptuous toward us. They've simply been talking their way through their explanations, without paying any attention to whether we were following them or were left behind.                                                                                  *b*

THT. What do you mean?

VIS. For heaven's sake, Theaetetus, do you understand anything of what they mean each time one of them says that many or one or two things *are* or *have become* or *are becoming*, or when another one speaks of hot mixed with cold and supposes that there are separations and combinations?[46] Earlier in my life I used to think I understood exactly what someone meant when he said just what we're confused about now, namely, this *is not*. You do see what confusion we're in about it?

THT. Yes, I do.                                                                         *c*

VIS. But just perhaps the very same thing has happened to us equally about *is*. We say we're in the clear about it, and that we understand when someone says it, but that we don't understand *is not*. But maybe we're in the same state about both.

THT. Maybe.

VIS. And let's suppose the same thing may be true of the other expressions we've just used.

THT. All right.

VIS. We can look into most of them later, if that seems to be the best thing to do. Now we'll think about the most fundamental and most important expression.                                                                          *d*

THT. Which one? Oh, obviously you're saying that *being* is the one we have to explore first—that we have to ask what people who say it think they're indicating by it.

VIS. You understand exactly, Theaetetus. I'm saying we have to follow the track this way. Let's ask—as if they were here—"Listen, you people who say that all things are just some two things, hot and cold or some such pair. What are you saying about them both when you say that they both *are* and each one *is*? What shall we take this *being* to be? Is it a third thing alongside those two beings, so that according to you everything is no longer two but three? Surely in calling one or the other of the two of       *e*

46. Like Cornford, I follow Rademacher in reading *allos eipei* for *allothi pei*.

them *being*, you aren't saying that they both are, since then in either case they'd be one and not two."

THT. That's true.

VIS. "But you do want to call both of them *being*?"

THT. Probably.

*244* VIS. "But," we'll say, "if you did that, friends, you'd also be saying very clearly that the two are one."

THT. That's absolutely right.

VIS. "Then clarify this for us, since we're confused about it. What do you want to signify when you say *being*? Obviously you've known for a long time. We thought we did, but now we're confused about it. So first teach it to us, so we won't think we understand what you're saying when just
*b* the contrary is the case." Would it be the least bit inappropriate for us to ask them this, and anyone else who says that everything is more than one?

THT. Not at all.

VIS. Well, then, shouldn't we do our best to find out from the people who say that everything is one what they mean by *being*?

THT. Of course.

VIS. Then they should answer this question: "Do you say that only one thing is?" "We do," they'll say, won't they?

THT. Yes.

VIS. "Well then, you call something *being*?"

THT. Yes.

*c* VIS. "Is that just what you call *one*, so that you use two names for the same thing? Or what?"

THT. How will they answer that question?

VIS. Obviously it's not the easiest thing in the world to answer that question—or any other question, either—for someone who makes the supposition that they do.

THT. Why not?

VIS. Surely it's absurd for someone to agree that there are two names when he maintains that there's only one thing.

THT. Of course.

VIS. And it's completely absurd, and unacceptable, for someone to say
*d* that there's a name if there's no account of it.[47]

THT. What do you mean?

VIS. If he supposes that a thing is different from its name, then surely he's mentioning two things.

---

47. Literally, if it has no *logos*, i.e., account or definition (cf. *supra*, n. 29).

THT. Yes.

VIS. And moreover if he supposes that the name is the same as the thing, he'll either be forced to say that the name is the name of nothing, or else, if he says that it's the name of something, then it's the name of nothing other than itself and so will turn out to be only the name of a name and nothing else.

THT. Yes.

VIS. And also *the one*, being the name of *the one*, will also be the one of the name.[48]

THT. It will have to be.

VIS. Well then, will they say that *the whole* is different from *the one being*, or the same as it?

THT. Of course they'll say it's the same, and they do.                    *e*

VIS. But suppose a whole is, as even Parmenides says,

All around like the bulk of a well-formed sphere,
Equal-balanced all ways from the middle, since neither anything
    more
Must it be, this way or that way, nor anything less.

If it's like that, then *that which is* will have a middle and extremities. And if it has those then it absolutely has to have parts, doesn't it?

THT. Yes.

VIS. But if a thing has parts then nothing keeps it from having the   *245* characteristic of being one in all its parts, and in that way it's all *being* and it's also *one whole*.

THT. Of course.

VIS. But something with that characteristic can't be just *the one* itself, can it?

THT. Why not?

VIS. Surely a thing that's truly one, properly speaking, has to be completely without parts.

THT. Yes.

---

48. The text here is corrupt, but the sense is (*contra* Cornford, p.222, n. 1) neither redundant nor unclear. The only thing that the text lacks is a finite verb in its main clause. Plato is relying on the thought that if the terms "one" and "name" designate one thing (in the sense that he assumes is relevant), then they are interchangeable, even to the point of generating the strange phrase "the one of the name."

*b*    VIS. But a thing like what we've described, which consists of many parts, won't fit that account.

THT. I understand.

VIS. Now if *that which is* has the characteristic of *the one* in this way, will it be one and a whole? Or shall we simply deny it's a whole at all?

THT. That's a hard choice.

VIS. You're right. If it has the characteristic of somehow being one, it won't appear to be the same as *the one*. Moreover, everything will then be more than one.

THT. Yes.

*c*    VIS. Further if *that which is* is not a whole by possessing that as a characteristic, but rather just is *the whole* itself, *that which is* will turn out to be less than itself.

THT. Certainly.

VIS. And because it's deprived of itself, *that which is* will be *not being*, according to that account.

THT. Yes.

VIS. And everything will be more than one, since *that which is* and *the whole* will each have its own separate nature.

THT. Yes.

VIS. But if *the whole* is not at all, then the very same things are true of
*d* *that which is*, and in addition to not being, it would not even become a being.

THT. Why not?

VIS. Invariably whatever becomes has at some point become as a whole. So we can't label either *being* or *becoming* as being without taking *the whole* to be among the beings too.

THT. That seems entirely right.

VIS. And moreover something that isn't a whole can't be of any quantity at all, since something that's of a certain quantity has to be a whole of that quantity, whatever it may be.

THT. Exactly.

VIS. And millions of other issues will also arise, each generating indefi-
*e* nitely many confusions, if you say that being is only two or one.

THT. The ones that just turned up show that. One problem led to another, and at each step there was more and more difficulty and uncertainty about what we'd just said at the previous stage.

VIS. We haven't gone through all the detailed accounts that people give of *that which is* and *that which is not*, but this is enough. Now we have to look at the people who discuss the issue in another way. Our aim is to

have them all in view and that way to see that saying what *that which is* is  246
isn't a bit easier than saying what *that which is not* is.

THT. So we need to go on to these people too.

VIS. It seems that there's something like a battle of gods and giants
among them, because of their dispute with each other over *being*.[49]

THT. How?

VIS. One group drags everything down to earth from the heavenly
region of the invisible, actually clutching rocks and trees with their hands.
When they take hold of all these things they insist that only what offers
tangible contact is, since they define *being* as the same as body. And if any     b
of the others say that something without a body is, they absolutely despise
him and won't listen to him any more.

THT. These are frightening men you're talking about. I've met quite a
lot of them already.

VIS. Therefore the people on the other side of the debate defend their
position very cautiously, from somewhere up out of sight. They insist
violently that true being is certain nonbodily forms that can be thought
about. They take the bodies of the other group, and also what they call
the truth, and they break them up verbally into little bits and call them a     c
process of coming-to-be instead of being. There's a never-ending battle
going on constantly between them about this issue.

THT. That's true.

VIS. Let's talk with each of these groups about the *being* that they posit.

THT. How shall we do it?

VIS. It's easier to talk with the ones who put *being* in the Forms. They're
gentler people. It's harder—and perhaps just about impossible—with the
ones who drag everything down to body by force. It seems to me that we     d
have to deal with them this way.

THT. Namely . . . ?

VIS. Mainly by making them actually better than they are—if we somehow could. But if we can't do that in fact, then let's do it in words, by
supposing that they're willing to answer less wildly than they actually do.
Something that better people agree to is worth more than what worse ones
agree to. Anyway we're not concerned with the people; we're looking for
what's true.

THT. That's absolutely right.     e

VIS. Then tell the better people to answer you and interpret what they say.

THT. All right.

49. See Hesiod, *Theogony*, esp. 675–715.

Vis. Then let them tell us this: do they say that anything is a mortal animal?

Tht. Of course they do.

Vis. And they agree that a mortal animal is an ensouled body?

Tht. Of course.

247 Vis. And so they're placing soul among the beings?

Tht. Yes.

Vis. What then? Do they say that this soul is just and that soul is unjust, and that this one's intelligent and that one isn't?

Tht. Of course.

Vis. But isn't a soul just by the possession of justice, and isn't another soul contrary to it by the possession and presence of the contrary?

Tht. Yes, they agree with that.

Vis. But they'll say further that at any rate what can be present to a thing or absent from it is something.

Tht. Yes.

b Vis. So since there is justice and intelligence and the rest of virtue, and also their contraries, and moreover since there is a soul in which those things come to be present, do they say that any of these are visible, or that they all are invisible?

Tht. They can hardly say any of them is visible.

Vis. And what about these invisible things? Do they say that they have bodies?

Tht. They don't give one single answer to that question. They do say that the soul seems to them to have a kind of body. But as far as intelligence and the other things you've asked about are concerned, they're ashamed

c and don't dare either to agree that they are not beings or to insist that everything is a body.

Vis. Obviously this breed of men has improved, Theaetetus. The native earthborn giants would never have been ashamed to hold the line for their position, that anything they can't squeeze in their hands is absolutely nothing.

Tht. That pretty much describes their thinking.

Vis. Then let's go back to questioning them. It's enough if they admit

d that even a small part of *that which is* doesn't have body. They need to say something about what's common to both it and the things that do have body, which they focus on when they say that they both *are*. Maybe that will raise some confusion for them. If it does, then think about whether they'd be willing to accept our suggestion that *that which is* is something like the following.

Tht. Like what? Tell me and maybe we'll know.

VIS. I'm saying that a thing really is if it has any capacity at all, either   *e*
by nature to do something to something else or to have even the smallest
thing done to it by even the most trivial thing, even if it only happens once.
I'll take it as a definition that[50] *those which are* amount to nothing other
than *capacity*.

THT. They accept that, since they don't have anything better to say
right now.

VIS. Fine. Maybe something else will occur to them later, and to us
too. For now let's agree with them on this much.   *248*

THT. All right.

VIS. Let's turn to the other people, the friends of the forms.[51] You serve
as their interpreter for us.

THT. All right.

VIS. You people distinguish coming-to-be and being and say that they
are separate? Is that right?

THT. "Yes."

VIS. And you say that by our bodies and through perception we have
dealings with coming-to-be, but we deal with real being by our souls and
through reasoning. You say that being always stays the same and in the
same state, but coming-to-be varies from one time to another.

THT. "We do say that."   *b*

VIS. And what shall we say this *dealing with* is that you apply in the two
cases? Doesn't it mean what we said just now?

THT. "What?"

VIS. What happens when two things come together, and by some capacity one does something to the other or has something done to it. Or maybe
you don't hear their answer clearly, Theaetetus. But I do, probably because
I'm used to them.

THT. Then what account do they give?

VIS. They don't agree with what we just said to the earth people about   *c*
being.

THT. What's that?

VIS. We took it[52] as a sufficient definition of *beings* that the capacity be
present in a thing to do something or have something done to it, to or by
even the smallest thing.

---

50. The text here is mildly questionable.

51. See n. 26, on 235d. Here Plato is obviously alluding to the sense of the term involved
in his doctrine of Forms as it appears in, for instance, the *Phaedo* and *Republic*.

52. In 247e.

THT. Yes.

VIS. In reply they say that coming-to-be has the capacity to do something or have something done to it, but that this capacity doesn't fit with being.

THT. Is there anything to that?

*d* VIS. We have to reply that we need them to tell us more clearly whether they agree that the soul knows and also that *being* is known.

THT. "Yes," they say.

VIS. Well then, do you say that knowing and being known are cases of doing, or having something done, or both? Is one of them doing and the other having something done? Or is neither a case of either?

THT. Obviously neither is a case of either, since otherwise they'd be saying something contrary to what they said before.

*e* VIS. Oh, I see. You mean that if knowing is doing something, then necessarily what is known has something done to it. When being is known by knowledge, according to this account, then insofar as it's known it's changed by having something done to it—which we say wouldn't happen to something that's at rest.

THT. That's correct.

VIS. But for heaven's sake, are we going to be convinced that it's true that change, life, soul, and understanding are not present in *that which* 249 *wholly is*, and that it neither lives nor thinks, but stays changeless, solemn, and holy, without any intelligence?

THT. If we did, sir, we'd be admitting something frightening.

VIS. But are we going to say that it has intelligence but doesn't have life?

THT. Of course not.

VIS. But are we saying that it has both those things in it while denying that it has them in its soul?

THT. How else would it have them?

VIS. And are we saying that it has intelligence, life, and soul, but that it's at rest and completely changeless even though it's alive?

*b* THT. All that seems completely unreasonable.

VIS. Then both *that which changes* and also *change* have to be admitted as being.

THT. Of course.

VIS. And so, Theaetetus, it turns out that if no beings change then nothing anywhere possesses any intelligence about anything.[53]

53. I accept Badham's conjecture here, inserting *panton* after *onton*.

THT. Absolutely not.

VIS. But furthermore if we admit that everything is moving and changing, then on that account we take the very same thing away from *those which are.*

THT. Why?

VIS. Do you think that without rest anything would be the same, in the same state in the same respects?

THT. Not at all.

VIS. Well then, do you see any case in which intelligence is or comes-to-be anywhere without these things?    *c*

THT. Not in the least.

VIS. And we need to use every argument we can to fight against anyone who does away with knowledge, understanding, and intelligence but at the same time asserts anything at all about anything.

THT. Definitely.

VIS. The philosopher—the person who values these things the most—absolutely has to refuse to accept the claim that everything is at rest, either from defenders of *the one* or from friends of the many forms. In addition    *d* he has to refuse to listen to people who say that *that which is* changes in every way. He has to be like a child begging for "both," and say that *that which is*—everything—comprises both *the unchanging* and *that which changes.*

THT. True.

VIS. Well now, apparently we've done a fine job of making our account pull together *that which is,* haven't we?

THT. Absolutely.

VIS. But for heaven's sake, Theaetetus, . . . Now I think we'll recognize how confused our investigation about it is.[54]

THT. Why, though? What do you mean?    *e*

VIS. Don't you notice, my young friend, that we're now in extreme ignorance about it, though it appears to us that we're saying something.

THT. It does to me anyway. But I don't completely understand how we got into this situation without noticing.

VIS. Then think more clearly about it. Given what we've just agreed to, would it be fair for someone to ask us the same question we earlier    *250* asked the people who say that everything is just *hot* and *cold?*[55]

THT. What was it? Remind me.

54. The text of this remark is garbled.
55. At 243d–244b.

VIS. Certainly. And I'll try, at any rate, to do it by asking you in just the same way as I asked them, so that we can move forward at the same pace.

THT. Good.

VIS. Now then, wouldn't you say that *change* and *rest* are completely contrary to each other?

THT. Of course.

VIS. And you'd say they both equally are, and that each of them is?

*b*    THT. Yes.

VIS. When you admit that they are, are you saying that both and each of them change?

THT. Not at all.

VIS. And are you signifying that they rest when you say that they both are?

THT. Of course not.

VIS. So do you conceive *that which is* as a third thing alongside them which encompasses *rest* and *change*? And when you say that they both are, are you taking the two of them together and focusing on their association with *being*?

*c*    THT. It does seem probably true that when we say *change* and *rest* are, we do have a kind of omen of *that which is* as a third thing.

VIS. So *that which is* isn't both *change* and *rest*; it's something different from them instead.[56]

THT. It seems so.

VIS. Therefore by its own nature *that which is* doesn't either rest or change.

THT. I suppose it doesn't.

VIS. Which way should someone turn his thoughts if he wants to establish for himself something clear about it?

THT. I don't know.

VIS. I don't think any line is easy. If something isn't changing, how can

*d*  it not be resting? And how can something not change if it doesn't in any way rest? But now *that which is* appears to fall outside both of them. Is that possible?[57]

THT. Absolutely not.

VIS. In this connection we ought to remember the following.

---

56. Cf. 249d.

57. Plato is arguing that that which is does not, simply by virtue of being that which is, either change or rest. This point, however, might seem to be confused with the claim that that which is neither changes nor rests. Cf. Introd., Sec. 3.

THT. What?

VIS. When we were asked what we should apply the name *that which is not* to, we became completely confused. Do you remember?

THT. Of course.

VIS. And now aren't we in just as much confusion about *that which is?*   *e*

THT. We seem to be in even more confusion, if that's possible.

VIS. Then we've now given a complete statement of our confusion. But there's now hope, precisely because both *that which is* and *that which is not* are involved in equal confusion. That is, in so far as one of them is clarified, either brightly or dimly, the other will be too. And if we can't  *251* see either of them, then anyway we'll push our account of both of them forward as well as we can.[58]

THT. Fine.

VIS. Let's give an account of how we call the very same thing, whatever it may be, by several names.

THT. What, for instance? Give me an example.

VIS. Surely we're speaking of a man even when we name him several things, that is, when we apply colors to him and shapes, sizes, defects, and virtues. In these cases and a million others we say that he's not only a man  *b* but also is good and indefinitely many different things. And similarly on the same account we take a thing to be one, and at the same time we speak of it as many by using many names for it.

THT. That's true.

VIS. Out of all this we've prepared a feast for young people and for old late-learners. They can grab hold of the handy idea that it's impossible for that which is many to be one and for that which is one to be many. They evidently enjoy forbidding us to say that a man is good, and only  *c* letting us say that that which is good is good, or that the man is a man. You've often met people, I suppose, who are carried away by things like that. Sometimes they're elderly people who are amazed at this kind of thing, because their understanding is so poor and they think they've discovered something prodigiously wise.

THT. Of course.

VIS. Then let's direct our questions now both to these people and also  *d* to the others we were talking with before. That way our account will be addressed to everyone who's ever said anything at all about *being*.[59]

---

58. Cornford translates, "force a passage through with both elbows at once" (see his p. 251, n. 1). The point is clearly that we need to understand both *that which is* and *that which is not*.

59. That is, Plato now proposes to fulfill the project announced at 245e–246a.

THT. What questions do you mean?

VIS. Shall we refuse to apply *being* to *change* or to *rest*, or anything to anything else? Shall we take these things to be unblended and incapable of having a share of each other in the things we say? Or shall we pull them all together and treat them all as capable of associating with each other? Or shall we say that some can associate and some can't? Which of these

e options shall we say they'd choose, Theaetetus?

THT. I don't know how to answer for them.

VIS. Why don't you reply to the options one by one by thinking about what results from each of them?

THT. Fine.

VIS. First, if you like, let's take them to say that nothing has any capacity at all for association with anything. Then *change* and *rest* won't have any share in *being*.

252 THT. No, they won't.

VIS. Well then, will either of them be, if they have no association with being?

THT. No.

VIS. It seems that agreeing to that destroys everything right away, both for the people who make everything change, for the ones who make everything an unchanging unit, and for the ones who say that beings are forms that always stay the same and in the same state. All of these people apply *being*. Some do it when they say that things really are changing, and others do it when they say that things really are at rest.

THT. Absolutely.

b VIS. Also there are people who put everything together at one time and divide them at another.[60] Some put them together into one and divide them into indefinitely many, and others divide them into a finite number of elements and put them back together out of them. None of these people, regardless of whether they take this to happen in stages or continuously, would be saying anything if there isn't any blending.

THT. Right.

VIS. But furthermore the most ridiculous account is the one that's adopted by the people who won't allow anything to be called by a name that it gets by association with something else.

c THT. Why?

VIS. They're forced to use *being* about everything, and also *separate*, *from others*, *of itself*, and a million other things. They're powerless to keep

---

60. These thinkers were introduced at 242c–d, e–243a.

from doing it—that is, from linking them together in their speech. So they don't need other people to refute them, but have an enemy within, as people say, to contradict them, and they go carrying him around talking in an undertone inside them like the strange ventriloquist Eurycles.[61]

THT. That's a very accurate comparison.    *d*

VIS. Well then, what if we admit that everything has the capacity to associate with everything else?

THT. I can solve that one.

VIS. How?

THT. Because if *change* and *rest* belonged to each other then *change* would be completely at rest and conversely *rest* itself would be changing.

VIS. But I suppose it's ruled out by very strict necessity that *change* should be at rest and that *rest* should change.[62]

THT. Of course.

VIS. So the third option is the only one left.

THT. Yes.

VIS. Certainly one of the following things has to be the case: either    *e* everything is willing to blend, or nothing is, or some things are and some are not.

THT. Of course.

VIS. And we found that the first two options were impossible.

THT. Yes.

VIS. So everyone who wants to give the right answer will choose the third.

THT. Absolutely.

VIS. Since some will blend and some won't, they'll be a good deal like    *253* letters of the alphabet. Some of them fit together with each other and some don't.

THT. Of course.

VIS. More than the other letters the vowels run through all of them like a bond, linking them together, so that without a vowel no one of the others can fit with another.

THT. Definitely.

VIS. So does everyone know which kinds of letters can associate with which, or does it take an expert?

THT. It takes an expert.

VIS. What kind?

---

61. See Aristophanes, *Wasps*, 1017–20.
62. Cf. n. 57, on 250d, and Introd., Sec. 3.

THT. An expert in grammar.

*b*  VIS. Well then, isn't it the same with high and low notes? The musician is the one with the expertise to know which ones mix and which ones don't, and the unmusical person is the one who doesn't understand that.

THT. Yes.

VIS. And in other cases of expertise and the lack of it we'll find something similar.

THT. Of course.

VIS. Well then, we've agreed that kinds mix with each other in the same way. So if someone's going to show us correctly which kinds harmonize with which and which kinds exclude each other, doesn't he have to have

*c*  some kind of knowledge as he proceeds through the discussion? And in addition doesn't he have to know whether there are any kinds that run through all of them and link them together to make them capable of blending, and also, when there are divisions, whether certain kinds running through wholes are always the cause of the division?

THT. Of course that requires knowledge—probably just about the most important kind.

VIS. So, Theaetetus, what shall we label this knowledge? Or for heaven's sake, without noticing have we stumbled on the knowledge that free people have? Maybe we've found the philosopher even though we were looking for the sophist?

THT. What do you mean?

*d*  VIS. Aren't we going to say that it takes expertise in dialectic to divide things by kinds and not to think that the same form is a different one or that a different form is the same?

THT. Yes.

VIS. So if a person can do that, he'll be capable of adequately discriminating a single form spread out all through a lot of others, each of which stands separate from the others. In addition he can discriminate forms that are different from each other but are included within a single form that's outside them, or a single form that's connected as a unit throughout many wholes, or many forms that are completely separate from others.

*e*  That's what it is to know how to discriminate by kinds how things can associate and how they can't.

THT. Absolutely.

VIS. And you'll assign this dialectical activity only to someone who has a pure and just love of wisdom.

THT. You certainly couldn't assign it to anyone else.

VIS. We'll find that the philosopher will always be in a location like this

if we look for him. He's hard to see clearly too, but not in the same way *254*
as the sophist.

THT. Why not?

VIS. The sophist runs off into the darkness of *that which is not*, which
he's had practice dealing with, and he's hard to see because the place is
so dark. Isn't that right?

THT. It seems to be.

VIS. But the philosopher always uses reasoning to stay near the form,
*being*. He isn't at all easy to see because that area is so bright and the eyes
of most people's souls can't bear to look at what's divine.                        *b*

THT. That seems just as right as what you just said before.

VIS. We'll think about the philosopher more clearly soon if we want to.
But as far as the sophist is concerned we obviously shouldn't give up until
we've gotten a good enough look at him.

THT. Fine.

VIS. We've agreed on this: some kinds will associate with each other
and some won't, some will to a small extent and others will associate a
great deal, and still others are all-pervading—nothing prevents them from    *c*
being associated with every one of them. So next let's pursue our account
together this way. Let's not talk about every form. That way we won't be
thrown off by dealing with too many of them. Instead let's choose some
of the most important ones. First we'll ask what they're like, and next we'll
ask about their ability to associate with each other. Even if our grasp of
*that which is* and *that which is not* isn't completely clear, our aim will be to
avoid being totally without an account of them—so far as that's allowed
by our present line of inquiry—and see whether we can get away with    *d*
saying that *that which is not* really is that which is not.

THT. That's what we have to do.

VIS. The most important kinds we've just been discussing are *that which
is*, *rest*, and *change*.

THT. Yes, by far.

VIS. And we say that two of them don't blend with each other.

THT. Definitely not.

VIS. But *that which is* blends with both of them, since presumably both
of them are.

THT. Of course.

VIS. We do have three of them.

THT. Yes.

VIS. So each of them is different from two of them, but is the same as
itself.

*e*     THT. Yes.

VIS. But what in the world are *the same* and *the different* that we've been speaking of? Are they two kinds other than those three but necessarily always blending with them? And do we have to think of them all as being 255 five and not three? Or have what we've been calling *the same* and *the different* turned out, without our realizing it, to be among those three?

THT. Maybe.

VIS. But change and rest are certainly not *different* or *the same*.

THT. Why not?

VIS. Whatever we call change and rest in common can't be either one of them.

THT. Why not?

VIS. Then change would rest and rest would change. For it's true of both, *different* and *the same*, that if it becomes either one of *change* or *rest*, *b* then it will force the other to change to the contrary of its own nature, since it will share in its contrary.

THT. Absolutely.

VIS. And both do share in *the same* and in *the different*.

THT. Yes.

VIS. Then anyway let's not say that change is *the same* or *the different*, nor that rest is.

THT. All right.

VIS. But do we have to think of *that which is* and *the same* as one thing?

THT. Maybe.

VIS. But if *that which is* and *the same* don't signify distinct things, then *c* when we say that *change* and *rest* both are, we'll be labeling both of them as being the same.

THT. But certainly that's impossible.

VIS. So it's impossible for *the same* and *that which is* to be one.

THT. I suppose so.

VIS. Shall we take *the same* as a fourth in addition to the other three forms?

THT. Of course.

VIS. Well then, do we have to call *the different* a fifth? Or should we think of it and *that which is* as two names for one kind?

THT. Maybe.

VIS. But I think you'll admit that some of *those which are* are said by themselves, but some are always said in relation to other things.

THT. Of course.

*d*     VIS. But *the different* always is in relation to another, isn't it?

THT. Yes.

VIS. But it wouldn't be if *that which is* and *the different* weren't completely distinct. If *the different* shared in both kinds[63] the way *that which is* does, then some of the things that are different would be different without being different in relation to anything different.[64] In fact, though, it turns out that whatever is different definitely has to be what it is *from* something that's different.

THT. That's exactly the way it is.

VIS. And we do have to call the nature of *the different* a fifth among the     *e*
forms we're choosing.

THT. Yes.

VIS. And we're going to say that it pervades all of them, since each of them is different from the others, not because of its own nature but because of sharing in the type of *the different*.

THT. Absolutely.

VIS. Let's take up each of the five one by one and say this.

THT. What?

VIS. First let's say that *change* is completely different from *rest*. Shall we say that?

THT. Yes.

VIS. So it is not *rest*.

THT. Not at all.

VIS. But it is, because it shares in *that which is*.                        *256*

THT. Yes.

VIS. Then again *change* is different from *the same*.

THT. Pretty much.

VIS. So it is not *the same*.

THT. No.

VIS. But still it was *the same*, we said,[65] because everything has a share of that.

THT. Definitely.

VIS. We have to agree without any qualms that *change* is *the same* and not *the same*. When we say that it's *the same* and not *the same*, we aren't speaking the same way. When we say it's *the same*, that's because it shares     *b*
in *the same* in relation to itself. But when we say it's not *the same*, that's

---

63. I.e., in both *said by themselves* and *said in relation to other things*, which Plato here (perhaps only by a manner of speaking) treats as forms.

64. That is, not in relation to anything different from them.

65. Cf. 255a.

because of its association with *the different*. Because of its association with *the different*, change is separated from *the same*, and so becomes not it but different. So that it's right to say that it's not *the same*.

THT. Of course.

VIS. So if *change* itself ever somehow had a share in *rest*, there would be nothing strange about labeling it *resting*?

THT. That's absolutely right, as long as we admit that some kinds will blend with each other and some won't.

c    VIS. That, though, we demonstrated earlier, before we came to this point, and we showed that by nature it has to be so.[66]

THT. Of course.

VIS. Let's say it again: *change* is different from *different*, just as it's other than both *the same* and *rest*.

THT. It has to be.

VIS. So in a way it is different and not different, according to what we've said.

THT. Right.

VIS. So what next? Are we going to say that *change* is different from the first three but not from the fourth, in spite of the fact that we've agreed

d    that there were five things we were going to investigate.

THT. How could we do that? We can't admit that there are fewer of them than there appeared to be just now.

VIS. So shall we go on fearlessly contending that *change* is different from *that which is*?

THT. Yes, we should be absolutely fearless.

VIS. So it's clear that *change* really is both something that is not, but also a thing that is since it partakes in *that which is*?

THT. That's absolutely clear.

VIS. So it has to be possible for *that which is not* to be, in the case of change and also of all the kinds. That's because for all of them the nature

e    of *the different* makes each of them not be, by making it different from *that which is*. And we're going to be right if we say that all of them *are not* in this same way. And on the other hand we're also going to be right if we call them beings, because they have a share in *that which is*.

THT. It seems that way.

VIS. So as applied to each of the forms *that which is* is extensive, and *that which is not* is indefinite in quantity.

THT. That seems right.

66. At 251a–252c.

Vis. So we have to say that *that which is* itself is different from the 257 others.

Tht. Necessarily.

Vis. So even *that which is* is not, precisely insofar as the others are, since, not being them, it is one thing, namely itself, and on the other hand it is those others, which are an indefinite number.

Tht. I suppose so.

Vis. So then we shouldn't even be annoyed about this conclusion, precisely because it's the nature of kinds to allow association with each other. And if somebody doesn't admit that, then he needs to win us over from our earlier line of argument for it,[67] in order to win us over from its consequences.

Tht. That's entirely fair.

Vis. Now let's look at this. *b*

Tht. What?

Vis. It seems that when we say *that which is not*, we don't say something contrary to *that which is*, but only something different from it.

Tht. Why?

Vis. It's like this. When we speak of something as *not large*, does it seem to you that we indicate *the small* rather than *the equal*?

Tht. Of course not.

Vis. So we won't agree with somebody who says that denial signifies a contrary. We'll only admit this much: when "not" and "non-" are prefixed *c* to names that follow them, they indicate something *other* than the names, or rather, other than the things to which the names following the negation are applied.

Tht. Absolutely.

Vis. If you don't mind, though, let's think about this.

Tht. What?

Vis. The nature of *the different* appears to be chopped up, just like knowledge.

Tht. Why?

Vis. Knowledge is a single thing, too, I suppose. But each part of it that belongs to something is marked off and has a name peculiar to itself. *d* That's why there are said to be many expertises and many kinds of knowledge.

Tht. Of course.

---

67. Esp. 244b–245d, 251a–253c.

Vis. And so the same thing happens to the parts of the nature of *the different*, too, even though it's one thing.

Tht. Maybe. But shall we say how?

Vis. Is there a part of *the different* that's placed over against *the beautiful?*

Tht. Yes.

Vis. Shall we say that it's nameless, or does it have a name?

Tht. It has a name. What we call *not beautiful* is the thing that's different from nothing other than the nature of the beautiful.

Vis. Now go ahead and tell me this.

*e*    Tht. What?

Vis. Isn't it in the following way that *the not beautiful* turns out to be, namely, by being both marked off within one kind of *those that are*,[68] and also set over against one of *those that are?*[69]

Tht. Yes.

Vis. Then it seems that *the not beautiful* is a sort of setting of a being over against a being.

Tht. That's absolutely right.

Vis. Well then, according to this account, is *the beautiful* more a being than *the not beautiful?*

Tht. Not at all.

*258*   Vis. So we have to say that both *the not large* and *the large* equally *are.*

Tht. Yes.

Vis. So we also have to put *the not just* on a par with *the just*, in that neither *is* any more than the other.

Tht. Of course.

Vis. And we'll speak about the others in the same way too, since the nature of *the different* appeared as being one of *those that are.* And because it *is*, we have to posit its parts as no less beings.[70]

Tht. Of course.

Vis. So it seems that the setting against each other of the nature of a
*b*  part of *the different* and the nature of a part of *that which is* is not any less being—if we're allowed to say such a thing—than *that which is* itself. And it does not signify something contrary to *that which is* but only something different from it.

Tht. Clearly.

---

68. I.e., within *the different*; that is, it is one of the "parts" of *the different*, and stands to it as the various parts of knowledge stand to knowledge.

69. I.e., over against *the beautiful*.

70. As per 257c–e.

Vis. So what shall we call it?

Tht. Obviously *that which is not*—which we were looking for because of the sophist—is just exactly this.

Vis. Then does it have just as much being as any of the others, as you said it did? Should we work up the courage now to say that *that which is not* definitely is something that has its own nature? Should we say that just as *the large* was large, *the beautiful* was beautiful, *the not large* was not large,          c
and *the not beautiful* was not beautiful, in the same way *that which is not* also was and is not being, and is one form among the many *that are*? Do we, Theaetetus, still have any doubts about that?

Tht. No.

Vis. You know, our disbelief in Parmenides has gone even farther than his prohibition.

Tht. How?

Vis. We've pushed our investigation ahead and shown him something even beyond what he prohibited us from even thinking about.

Tht. In what way?

Vis. Because he says, remember,[71]          d

Never shall it force itself on us, that that which is not may be;
Keep your thought Far away from this path of searching.

Tht. That's what he says.

Vis. But we've not only shown that *those which are not* are. We've also caused what turns out to be the form of *that which is not* to appear. Since we showed that the nature of *the different* is, chopped up among all beings          e
in relation to each other, we dared to say that *that which is not* really is just this, namely, each part of the nature of *the different* that's set over against *that which is*.

Tht. And what we've said seems to me completely and totally true.

Vis. Nobody can say that this *that which is not*, which we've made to appear and now dare to say is, is the contrary of *that which is*. We've said good-bye long ago to any contrary of *that which is*, and to whether it is or          259
not, and also to whether or not an account can be given of it. With regard to *that which is not*, which we've said is, let someone refute us and persuade us that we've made a mistake—or else, so long as he can't do that, he should say just what we say. He has to say that the kinds blend with each other, that *that which is* and *the different* pervade all of them and each other,

71. Cf. n. 28, on 237a.

that *the different* shares in *that which is* and so, because of that sharing, is. But he won't say that it is that which it shares in, but that it is different from it, and necessarily, because it *is* different from *that which is*, it clearly

*b* can be *what is not*. On the other hand *that which is* has a share in *the different*, so, being different from all of the others, it is not each of them and it is not all of the others except itself. So *that which is* indisputably is not millions of things, and all of the others together, and also each of them, are in many ways and also are not in many ways.

THT. True.

VIS. And if anyone doesn't believe these contrarieties, he has to think about them himself and say something better than what we've said. But if

*c* he thinks he's recognized a problem in it and enjoys dragging the argument back and forth, then he's been carried away by something that's not worth much of anyone's attention—to go by what we've just been saying, anyway. A thing like that isn't clever or hard to discover, but the other thing is both difficult and at the same time beautiful.

THT. What other thing?

VIS. The thing we said earlier. That is, we should leave pointless things like this alone.[72] Instead we should be able to follow what a person says and scrutinize it step by step. When he says that what's different is the same in a certain way or that what's the same is different in a certain way,

*d* we should understand just what way he means, and the precise respect in which he's saying that the thing is the same or different. But when someone makes that which is the same appear different in just any old way, or vice versa, or when he makes what's large appear small or something that's similar appear dissimilar—well, if someone enjoys constantly trotting out contraries like that in discussion, that's not true refutation. It's only the obvious new-born brain-child of someone who just came into contact with *those which are*.

THT. Definitely.

VIS. In fact, my friend, it's inept to try to separate everything from

*e* everything else. It's the sign of a completely unmusical and unphilosophical person.

THT. Why?

VIS. To dissociate each thing from everything else is to destroy totally everything there is to say. The weaving together of forms is what makes speech possible for us.

THT. That's true.

---

72. The text here is slightly garbled.

Vis. Think about what a good moment we picked to fight it out against *260*
people like that, and to force them further to let one thing blend with
another.

Tht. Why a good moment?

Vis. For speech's being one kind among *those that are.* If we were
deprived of that, we'd be deprived of philosophy—to mention the most
important thing. Besides, now we have to agree about what speech is, but
we'd be able to say nothing if speech were taken away from us and weren't
anything at all. And it would be taken away if we admitted that there's no *b*
blending of anything with anything else.

Tht. This last thing is right, anyway. But I don't understand why we
have to agree about speech.

Vis. Well, perhaps you'll understand if you follow me this way.

Tht. Where?

Vis. *That which is not* appeared to us to be one kind among others, but
scattered over all *those which are.*[73]

Tht. Yes.

Vis. So next we have to think about whether it blends with belief and
speech.

Tht. Why?

Vis. If it doesn't blend with them then everything has to be true. But *c*
if it does then there will be false belief and false speech, since falsity in
thinking and speaking amount to believing and saying *those that are not.*

Tht. Yes.

Vis. And if there's falsity then there's deception.

Tht. Of course.

Vis. And if there's deception then necessarily the world will be full of
copies, likenesses, and appearances.

Tht. Of course.

Vis. We said that the sophist had escaped into this region, but that he
denied that there has come to be or is such a thing as falsity. For he denied *d*
that anyone either thinks or says *that which is not,* on the ground that *that
which is not* never in any way has a share in *being.*

Tht. That's what he said.

Vis. But now it apparently does share in *that which is,* so they probably
wouldn't still put up a fight about that. Perhaps, though, he might say that
some forms share in *that which is not* and some don't, and that speech and
belief are ones that don't. So he might contend again that copy-making

73. See 257c, 258d–e.

*e* and appearance-making—in which we said he was contained—totally are not. His ground would be that belief and speech don't associate with *that which is not,* and that without this association falsity totally is not. That's why we have to search around for speech, belief, and appearance, and first discover what they are, so that when they appear we see their association

261 with *that which is not* clearly. Then when we've seen that clearly we can show that falsity is, and when we've shown that we can tie the sophist up in it, if we can keep hold of him—or else we'll let him go and look for him in another kind.

THT. What you said at the start seems absolutely true. The sophist is a hard kind to hunt down. He seems to have a whole supply of roadblocks, and whenever he throws one down in our way we have to fight through it before we can get to him. But now when we've barely gotten through the one about how *that which is not* is not, he's thrown another one down and

*b* we have to show that falsity is present in both speech and belief. And next, it seems, there will be another and another after that. A limit, it seems, never appears.

VIS. Even if you can only make a little progress, Theaetetus, you should cheer up. If you give up in this situation, what will you do some other time when you don't get anywhere or even are pushed back? A person like that

*c* would hardly capture a city, as the saying goes. But since we've done what you just said, my friend, the largest wall may already have been captured and the rest of them may be lower and easier.

THT. Fine.

VIS. Then let's take up speech and belief, as we said just now. That way we can calculate whether *that which is not* comes into contact with them, or whether they're both totally true and neither one is ever false.

THT. All right.

*d* VIS. Come on, then. Let's think about names again, the same way as we spoke about forms and letters of the alphabet. What we're looking for seems to lie in that direction.

THT. What kind of question about them do we have to answer?

VIS. Whether they all fit with each other, or none of them do, or some of them will and some of them won't.

THT. Anyway it's clear that some will and some won't.

VIS. Maybe you mean something like this: names that indicate some-

*e* thing when you say them one after another fit together, and names that don't signify anything when you put them in a row don't fit.

THT. What do you mean?

VIS. The same thing I thought you were assuming when you agreed with me just now—since there are two ways to use your voice to indicate something about being.

THT. What are they?

VIS. One kind is called *names*, and the other is called *verbs*. 262

THT. Tell me what each of them is.

VIS. A verb is the sort of indication that's applied to an action.

THT. Yes.

VIS. And a name is the kind of spoken sign that's applied to things that perform the actions.

THT. Definitely.

VIS. So no speech[74] is formed just from names spoken in a row, and also not from verbs that are spoken without names.

THT. I didn't understand that.

VIS. Clearly you were focusing on something else when you agreed *b* with me just now. What I meant was simply this: things don't form speech if they're said in a row like this.

THT. Like what?

VIS. For example, "walks runs sleeps," and other verbs that signify actions. Even if somebody said all of them one after another that wouldn't be speech.

THT. Of course not.

VIS. Again, if somebody said "lion stag horse," and whatever names there are of things that perform actions, the series wouldn't make up speech. The *c* sounds he uttered in the first or second way wouldn't indicate either an action or an inaction or the being of something that is or of something that is not—not until he mixed verbs with nouns. But when he did that, they'd fit together and speech—the simplest and smallest kind of speech, I suppose—would arise from that first weaving of name and verb together.

THT. What do you mean?

VIS. When someone says "man learns," would you say that's the shortest and simplest kind of speech?

THT. Yes. *d*

---

74. "Speech" throughout this section translates the word *logos* (on which see n. 29, *supra*). Plato uses the word here so that a single word by itself does not count as *logos*. One might wish to translate the word by "sentence" or "statement." That, however, would be too narrow, because Plato uses *logos* in a much broader way. Just for example, in 268b Plato speaks of "long *logoi*" and "short *logoi*" but clearly is not talking about long and short sentences. The *logoi* that he deals with in this passage are mainly sentences (because he is dealing with problems about falsity of sentences and judgments), but *logos* itself does not simply mean "sentence."

VIS. Since he gives an indication about what is, or comes to be, or has come to be, or is going to be. And he doesn't just name, but *accomplishes* something, by weaving verbs with names. That's why we said he speaks and doesn't just name. In fact this weaving is what we use the word "speech" for.

THT. Right.

VIS. So some things fit together and some don't. Likewise some vocal
*e* signs don't fit together, but the ones that do produce speech.

THT. Absolutely.

VIS. But there's still this small point.

THT. What?

VIS. Whenever there's speech it has to be about something. It's impossible for it not to be about something.

THT. Yes.

VIS. And speech also has to have some particular quality.

THT. Of course.

VIS. Now let's turn our attention to ourselves.

THT. All right.

VIS. I'll produce some speech by putting a thing together with an action by means of a name and a verb. You have to tell me what it's about.

*263*       THT. I'll do it as well as I can.

VIS. "Theaetetus sits." That's not a long piece of speech, is it?

THT. No, medium.

VIS. Your job is to tell what it's about, what it's of.

THT. Clearly it's about me, of me.

VIS. Then what about this one?

THT. What one?

VIS. "Theaetetus (to whom I'm now talking) flies".

THT. No one would ever deny that it's of me and about me.

VIS. We also say that each piece of speech has to have some particular quality.

*b*       THT. Yes.

VIS. What quality should we say each one of these has?

THT. The second one is false, I suppose, and the other one is true.

VIS. And the true one says *those that are*, as they are, about you.[75]

---

75. This sentence is multiply ambiguous, in a manner that is generated by two syntactic ambiguities. 1) First, the Greek here uses an idiom that English does not contain: which can be translated either by "says those that are, as they are" or "says those that are, that they are" (cf. 263d). "Those that are" is grammatically the direct object of "says," and "that/as (*hos*) they are" is added, as it were, epexegetically. The difference between "that" and "as" as translations of *hos* reflects an important syntactic ambiguity in the Greek construction.

THT. Of course.

VIS. And the false one says things different from *those that are*.

THT. Yes.

VIS. So it says *those that are not*, but that they are.[76]

THT. I suppose so.

VIS. But they're different things that are from the things that are about you—since we said that many beings are about you, and many are not.

THT. Absolutely.

VIS. In the first place, the second piece of speech I said about you must be one of the shortest there is, according to our definition of speech.  *c*

THT. We agreed to that just now, anyway.

VIS. And we agreed that it's of something.

THT. Yes.

VIS. And if it is not of you, it isn't of anything else.

THT. Of course not.

VIS. And if it were not of anything it would not be speech at all, since we showed that it was impossible for speech that is to be speech that is of nothing.

THT. Absolutely right.

VIS. But if someone says things about you, but says different things as  *d* the same or not beings as beings, then it definitely seems that false speech really and truly arises from that kind of putting together of verbs and names.

THT. Yes, very true.

VIS. Well then, isn't it clear by now that both true and false thought and belief and appearance can occur in our souls?

THT. How?

VIS. The best way for you to know how is for you first to grasp what they are and how they're different from each other.  *e*

THT. Then just tell me.

VIS. Aren't thought and speech the same, except that what we call thought is speech that occurs without the voice, inside the soul in conversation with itself?

THT. Of course.

---

I think that "as" probably gives the right idea here, but the question is murky.

2) The additional explanatory phrase, "about you," is also used with ambiguous syntax. "About you" can be taken to go with "says," with "are," or with both.

76. Here the syntax is the same as just above, except that the phrase "about you" is dropped, though perhaps it is to be taken as tacitly understood.

Vis. And the stream of sound from the soul that goes through the mouth is called speech?

Tht. Right.

Vis. And then again we know that speech contains . . .

Tht. What?

Vis. Affirmation and denial.

Tht. Yes.

264 Vis. So when affirmation or denial occurs as silent thought inside the soul, wouldn't you call that belief?

T.iT. Of course.

Vis. And what if that doesn't happen on its own but arises for someone through perception? When that happens, what else could one call it correctly, besides *appearance*?

Tht. Yes.

Vis. So since there is true and false speech, and that includes thinking, which appeared to be the soul's conversation with itself, and belief, which
b is the conclusion of thinking, and since we call *appearing* the blending of perception and belief, it follows that since these are all the same kind of thing as speech, some of them must sometimes be false.

Tht. Of course.

Vis. So you realize we've found false belief and speech sooner than we expected to just now. Then we were afraid that to look for it would be to attack a completely hopeless project.

Tht. Yes.

Vis. So let's not be discouraged about what's still left. Since these other
c things have come to light, let's remember the divisions of forms we made earlier.

Tht. Which ones?

Vis. We divided copy-making into two forms, likeness-making and appearance-making.

Tht. Yes.

Vis. And we said we were confused about which one to put the sophist in.

Tht. Yes.

Vis. And in our confusion about that we plunged into even greater bewilderment, when an account emerged that disagreed with everyone, by denying that there are likenesses or copies or appearances at all, on the
d ground that there isn't ever any falsity in any way anywhere.

Tht. That's right.

Vis. But now since false speech and false belief both appear to be, it's possible for imitations of *those that are* to be, and for expertise in deception to arise from that state of affairs.

THT. Yes.

VIS. And we agreed before that the sophist does fall under one of the two types we just mentioned.

THT. Yes.

VIS. Then let's try again to take the kind we've posited and cut it in two. Let's go ahead and always follow the righthand part of what we've *e* cut, and hold onto things that the sophist is associated with until we strip away everything that he has in common with other things. Then when we've left his own peculiar nature, let's display it, especially to ourselves but also to people to whom this sort of procedure is naturally congenial. *265*

THT. All right.

VIS. Didn't we begin by dividing expertise into productive and acquisitive?

THT. Yes.

VIS. And under the acquisitive part the sophist appeared in hunting, combat, wholesaling, and types of that sort.[77]

THT. Of course.

VIS. But now, since he's included among experts in imitation, first we obviously have to divide productive expertise in two. We say imitation is a sort of production, but of copies and not of the things themselves. Is *b* that right?

THT. Absolutely.

VIS. First of all, production has two parts.

THT. What are they?

VIS. Divine and human.

THT. I don't understand yet.

VIS. If you remember how we started,[78] we said production was any capacity that causes things to come to be that previously were not.

THT. I remember.

VIS. Take animals and everything mortal, including plants and every- *c* thing on the earth that grows from seeds and roots, and also all lifeless bodies made up inside the earth, whether fusible or not. Are we going to say that anything besides the craftsmanship of a god makes them come to be after previously not being? Or shall we rely on the saying and the widespread belief that . . . ?

77. See 221c–224e.
78. See 219b.

THT. That what?

VIS. Are we going to say that nature produces them by some spontane-ous cause that generates them without any thought, or by a cause that works by reason and divine knowledge derived from a god?

*d*  THT. I often shift back and forth on that from one view to the other, maybe because of my age. When I'm focusing on you now, and supposing that you think they come to be by the agency of a god, that's what I think too.

VIS. Fine, Theaetetus. If we thought you were the kind of person who might believe something different in the future we'd try to use some cogent, persuasive argument to make you agree. But since I know what *e*  your nature is and I know, too, that even without arguments from us it will tend in the direction that it's pulled toward now, I'll let the issue go. It would take too much time. I'll assume divine expertise produces the things that come about by so-called nature, and that human expertise produces the things that humans compound those things into. According to this account there are two kinds of production, human and divine.

THT. Right.

VIS. Since there are two of them, cut each of them in two again.

THT. How?

*266*  VIS. It's as if you'd already cut production all the way along its width, and now you'll cut it along its length.

THT. All right.

VIS. That way there are four parts of it all together, two human ones related to us and two divine ones related to the gods.

THT. Yes.

VIS. Then if we take the division we made the first way, one part of each of those parts is the production of originals. Just about the best thing to call the two parts that are left might be "copy-making." That way, production is divided in two again.

*b*  THT. Tell me again how each of them is divided.

VIS. We know that we human beings and the other living things, and also fire, water, and things like that, which natural things comes from, are each generated and produced by a god. Is that right?

THT. Yes.

VIS. And there are copies of each of these things, as opposed to the things themselves, that also come about by divine workmanship.

THT. What kinds of things?

VIS. Things in dreams, and appearances that arise by themselves during the day. They're shadows when darkness appears in firelight, and they're *c*  reflections when a thing's own light and the light of something else come together around bright, smooth surfaces and produce an appearance that looks the reverse of the way the thing looks from straight ahead.

THT. Yes, those are two products of divine production—the things themselves and the copies corresponding to each one.

VIS. And what about human expertise? We say housebuilding makes a house itself and drawing makes a different one, like a human dream made for people who are awake.

THT. Of course.         *d*

VIS. And just the same way in other cases, too, there are pairs of products of human production, that is, the thing itself, we say, and the copy.

THT. Now I understand better and I take it that there are two kinds of double production, divine and human in each division. One kind produces things themselves, and the other kind produces things similar to them.

VIS. Let's recall that one part of copy-making is likeness-making. The other kind was going to be appearance-making, if falsity appeared to be truly falsity and by nature one of *those that are*.       *e*

THT. Yes, it was.

VIS. But falsity did turn out that way, so are we going to count likeness-making and appearance-making as indisputably two forms?

THT. Yes.

VIS. Then let's divide appearance-making in two again.       *267*

THT. How?

VIS. Into one sort that's done with tools and one that uses one's own self as the tool of the person making the appearance.

THT. What do you mean?

VIS. When somebody uses his own body or voice to make something similar to your body or voice, I think the best thing to call this part of appearance-making is "imitating."

THT. Yes.

VIS. Let's set this part off by calling it imitation, and let's be lazy and let the other part go. We'll leave it to someone else to bring it together       *b* into a unit and give it a suitable name.

THT. All right, let's take the one and let the other go.

VIS. But the right thing, Theaetetus, is still to take imitation to have two parts. Think about why.

THT. Tell me.

VIS. Some imitators know what they're imitating and some don't. And what division is more important than the one between ignorance and knowledge?

THT. None.

VIS. Wasn't the imitation that we just mentioned the kind that's associated with knowledge? Someone who knew you and your character might imitate you, mightn't he?

*c* THT. Of course.

VIS. What about the character of justice and all of virtue taken together? Don't many people who are ignorant of it, but have some beliefs about it, try hard to cause what they believe it is to appear to be present in them. And don't they imitate it in their words and actions as much as they can?

THT. Very many people do that.

VIS. And are they all unsuccessful at seeming to be just without being just at all? Or is the opposite true?

THT. Yes, the opposite.

*d* VIS. I think we have to say that this person, who doesn't know, is a very different imitator from the previous one, who does.

THT. Yes.

VIS. Where would you get a suitable name for each of them? Isn't it obviously hard to, just because the people who came before us were thoughtless and lazy about dividing kinds into types, and so they never even tried to divide them. That's why we necessarily lack a good supply of names. Still, even though it sounds daring let's distinguish them by

*e* calling imitation accompanied by belief "belief-mimicry" and imitation accompanied by knowledge "informed mimicry."

THT. All right.

VIS. Then we need to use the former term, since the sophist isn't one of the people who know but is one of the people who imitate.

THT. He certainly is.

VIS. Let's examine the belief-mimic the way people examine iron, to see whether it's sound or has a crack in it.

THT. All right.

*268* VIS. Well, it has a big one. One sort of belief-mimic is foolish and thinks he knows the things he only has beliefs about. The other sort has been around a lot of discussions, and so by temperament he's suspicious and fearful that he doesn't know the things that he pretends in front of others to know.

THT. There definitely are both types that you've mentioned.

VIS. Shall we take one of these to be a sort of sincere imitator and the other to be an insincere one?

THT. That seems right.

VIS. And are there one or two kinds of insincere ones?

THT. You look and see.

VIS. I'm looking, and there clearly appear to be two. I see that one sort b can maintain his insincerity in long speeches to a crowd, and the other uses short speeches in private conversation to force the person talking with him to contradict himself.

THT. You're absolutely right.

VIS. How shall we show up the long-winded sort, as a statesman or as a demagogue?

THT. A demogogue.

VIS. And what shall we call the other one? Wise, or a sophist?

THT. We can't call him wise, since we took him not to know anything. But since he imitates the wise man he'll obviously have a name derived c from the wise man's name. And now at last I see that we have to call him the person who is really and truly a *sophist*.

VIS. Shall we weave his name together from start to finish and tie it up the way we did before?

THT. Of course.

VIS. Imitation of the contrary-speech-producing, insincere and un-knowing sort, of the appearance-making kind of copy-making, the word-juggling part of production that's marked off as human and not divine. Anyone who says the sophist is of this "blood and family"[79] will be saying, it seems, the complete truth.

THT. Absolutely.

79. See Homer, *Iliad* 6.211.